YOU ARE THE MESSAGE

Roger Ailes

with Jon Kraushar

CROWN
BUSINESS
NEW YORK

For Norma, Mom, and Joe

Published in the United States by Crown Business, an imprint
of the Crown Publishing Group, a division of Random
House, Inc., New York.

www.crownpublishing.com

CROWN BUSINESS is a trademark and CROWN and the Rising Sun
colophon are registered trademarks of Random House, Inc.

Originally published in the United States by Currency Books, an
imprint of the Doubleday Publishing Group, a division of
Random House, Inc., New York, in 1988 and 1995.

Crown Business books are available at special discounts for bulk
purchases for sales promotions or corporate use. Special editions,
including personalized covers, excerpts of existing books, or books
with corporate logos, can be created in large quantities for special
needs. For more information, contact Premium Sales at
(212) 572-2232 or e-mail specialmarkets@randomhouse.com.

Library of Congress Cataloging-in-Publication Data
Ailes, Roger.
  You are the message
  Roger Ailes with Jon Kraushar.
    p. cm.
  Bibliography: p.
  Includes index.
  1. Oral communication. I. Kraushar, Jon.
  II. Title.
P95.A35 1989   89-32219
302.2'24—dc20   CIP

ISBN 978-0-385-26542-3
PRINTED IN THE UNITED STATES OF AMERICA

35 34 33 32 31 30 29 28

CONTENTS

ACKNOWLEDGMENTS

This book is more than a recent venture. It's the result of a lifetime of learning. I'd like to acknowledge many of the people who have contributed to that learning process and to this book.

First, I'd like to thank J. McLain Stewart, Norma Ailes, Bill Mattasoni, Larry McCarthy, John Huddy, Kathy Ardleigh, and Kevin Hall for their time and ideas. I'd also like to thank corporate speechwriter Ron Nelson for his assistance, as well as Raymond Kraftson and Graeme Howard for their ongoing support and advice.

My thanks to Debi Daly and Ileana Guinot for their help and dedication.

A personal note of thanks to my mom for teaching me to set goals, and to my dad for teaching me to never quit—and to find the humor in life. Special thanks are also due to Joe Urban for his insight, research, and knowledge of communications and to Marje Ailes for her early encouragement and support.

And, finally, my appreciation to my collaborator and colleague, Jon Kraushar, without whom this book would not have been written.

ROGER AILES

PREFACE

The passage of a few years and the benefit of experience continue to prove that the principles of this book are timeless and that they work for everyone, regardless of gender, age, status, political affiliation, or nationality. Just after *You Are the Message* was first published, the book's ideas were subjected to a public trial by fire when I served as the senior media adviser to Vice President Bush's successful 1988 presidential campaign. In that campaign, I worked with George Bush on the skills you can read about here: how to effectively combine your substance and style to get what you want by being who you are, at your best.

By 1991, I had retired from political consulting to concentrate on my work with corporate and entertainment clients. I thus removed myself from involvement in the 1992 presidential campaign. However, one of Bill Clinton's top advisers admitted on television that he had read *You Are the Message*, and I understand the book had also been read by a number of Clinton's strategists.

Out of the glare of the headlines, I heard from many people who said that *You Are the Message* had made a difference in their lives. One woman called me from the airport in St. Louis, Missouri, and told me that the book had saved her career. She had been paralyzed with fear before a very important business presentation but had gained confidence and learned helpful techniques while reading the book during her flight.

Thank-you letters came from recent graduates who had found employment using the interviewing tips in this book. Business leaders called to order, in bulk, copies of the book to inspire and instruct their sales forces.

Members of the clergy wrote to say that their sermons had additional sparkle because of suggestions in *You Are the Message*. Several schools and colleges added the book to required reading lists. In fact, my niece, a college student in Toledo, Ohio, was told by a professor that she'd better read *You Are the Message*, and he asked if she had heard of the author. "Yes," she said proudly, "he's my uncle."

You Are the Message has been translated into foreign languages. However, I've been told that the English version was used to help Eastern European entrepreneurs and government officials communicate better in their new, free-market economies after the fall of Communism.

As I've often said, my interest in communication began with a quest to understand how and why audiences react. It is my hope that as a result of reading *You Are the Message*, many people will increase their understanding of the "composite messages" of others—friends and foes alike. People whose messages need to be carefully analyzed include politicians, journalists, business leaders, customers, competitors, family members, teachers, public officials, and everyone else capable of changing our lives. When you think about it, that includes anyone.

It is only through study and application that we can develop the capability and control needed to be intelligent speakers and —equally important—intelligent listeners. It is only through knowledge and discussion that we can sharpen our critical judgment, to distinguish between messengers who are harmful versus those who are beneficial. The message behind *You Are the Message* is: Take responsibility for the communication you send and the communication you receive. If there's misunderstanding either way, assume the responsibility for correcting it. Be a proactive—not a reactive—communicator. This book teaches you how to do that.

In 1993, I turned day-to-day management of my company, Ailes Communications, over to Jon Kraushar, my longtime colleague and collaborator on this book, because I was offered a challenge too big to pass up. I was asked to run the NBC-owned cable television company CNBC and to design and launch a new all-talk network, America's Talking, which I did on July 4, 1994. I remain associated with Ailes Communications as its founder, and Jon continues to teach the Ailes Method, as it is explained in *You Are the Message*. But, in returning full-time to an early passion of mine—television production—I have new opportunities to observe and apply the lessons of this book.

Today, more than ever, we see that television, mass media, and the blooming of the Information Age have changed the way we communicate. For better and worse, we live in an age of exposure where electronic media can record, monitor, and broadcast our thoughts and actions. Whether we like it or not, society's views of people and ideas are shaped and influenced by the flickering images on television and other electronic screens worldwide, carrying video, text, and sound. It can be breathtaking, exhilarating, or frightening to watch the impact and speed of the changes wrought by those images dancing across the monitors. We have seen political systems crumble or emerge, countries collapse or form, and personal fortunes soar or crash in, literally, seconds—just as long as it took to communicate.

As it says in this book, it takes only seven seconds for you to make an impression on other people. Ours is an era in which both information and interpretation keep getting more tightly compressed. That seven seconds is crucial in the making and breaking of impressions, relationships, sales, and decisions that affect the direction of our lives. Again, like it or not, a communication symbol of our age is the easily distracted, time-stressed television viewer using a remote control device to "channel surf" from program to program—from personality to personality—in mere seconds, in search of some gratifying mix of entertainment, inspiration, and information. That same restless, opportunistic viewer mentality confronts each of us as we present ourselves and our ideas to audiences small and large. *You Are the Message* is your guide for keeping others tuned in, to you.

Throughout the years, I have been a television producer, a frequent news source, and a commentator on issues including politics, entertainment, culture, and effective communication. But in 1994, I took on a new role. I became the host of a program on America's Talking, called "Straight Forward," where I interview interesting personalities from all walks of life.

I've thus come full circle in my career—from the coach to the presenter, from the man behind the camera to the man in front. Like all of us, I am subject to the rules and rewards described in this book. I occasionally stumble, and when I do, I review the principles of *You Are the Message*. I hope you enjoy this book and profit from it—by being who you really are, at your best.

Roger Ailes
March 1995

PREFACE
TO THE FIRST EDITION

The world has changed. So has the way we communicate. Those who fail to adapt will be left behind. But for those who want to succeed, there is only one secret:

YOU ARE THE MESSAGE.

That is the subject of this book.

This book is different from anything you may have heard or read about communications. The most exciting—and revolutionary—information in this book is that to be a good communicator you don't have to do tedious drills or alter your basic personality. We'll show you that you already have within you the tools to persuade and influence other people who are important to you, whether in your professional or personal life. Together we'll examine what I call the composite you. That composite makes up the total message you send to others, and it includes: the words you use, your voice, the way you move, the signals you send with your facial expressions, and your attitude.

Among the things we'll cover:

- How television has changed all the rules of communications and why it affects you more than you think
- How other people see you
- The four communications errors that your listeners won't forgive
- Breaking through fear and other performance blocks

- A few simple rules to insure speaking success in every situation
- Who some of the master communicators are—and how they do it
- How you can get what you want by being who you are

1
THE FIRST SEVEN SECONDS

It occurred to me as the last iron door clanged shut behind me: "Nobody's ever going to break out of this place." Ten minutes later, in prison, I was face-to-face with Charles Manson, the cult leader serving nine life sentences for his role in what some consider the most gruesome and bizarre murders in history—the killings of actress Sharon Tate and six others.

It was 1981 and I was executive producer of NBC–TV's "Tomorrow Coast to Coast," starring Tom Snyder and Rona Barrett. Segment producer Shelley Ross had arranged for Tom to conduct the first network interview with Manson in thirteen years. Manson was housed in a maximum security prison for the criminally insane at Vacaville, California.

I had read all the books and background about Manson but was unsure of exactly how the interview would go. I knew that we were dealing with a person who was, at best, completely crazy.

The idea of the interview itself was controversial. Many people felt Manson should not be interviewed—should not be granted a public forum. Other people felt that since he was kept alive after California passed the "no death penalty" law, we might learn something by interviewing and studying this type of person. I had mixed emotions, but my job was to get the interview.

When we entered the prison, we were led through a labyrinth of steel gates and cement block hallways until we ended up in a holding cell about twelve by fifteen feet. Across the hall from the holding cell was the prison library. The guards asked Tom to wait in the library while they brought Manson up. In the meantime, Tom and I sat down and discussed the interview at some length. We had several general questions but knew that the discussion would take on a life of its own once Manson started to ramble. The camera crew was setting up in the holding cell, so I decided to leave Tom, walk across the hall, and make sure the camera angles and lighting were right before Manson arrived.

As I walked out of the prison library and made a right turn, I bumped directly into someone. My eyes focused as this person bounced off my chest. From a distance of six inches I was staring directly into the eyes of Charles Manson. He was small, wiry, and mangy. He looked like a quick, dangerous ferret. I was momentarily shocked. As our eyes locked, I at first said nothing. I realized that a very primitive confrontation and mutual assessment were taking place. Then I said, "Mr. Manson, I'm in charge of this interview. I'd like you to come with me." For a split second more he stared at me. Then he lowered his head, backed away, and suddenly acted very obsequious. He was happy to meet me, he said, and wanted to know what I would like him to do.

In that first five to seven seconds, we had tested each other. I knew he loved to puff himself up like the Wizard of Oz and frighten people around him into doing what he wanted them to do. Since I didn't budge, he backed off and lowered his head, much as a dog does. They say a dog tests you by coming at you, fangs bared, head and tail up, and if you continue to show no fear, he will back off. Humans do this in their own way. Charles Manson was like a junkyard dog. Once he backed away, I knew I had control for the rest of the day. Tom did an excellent interview, although Manson occasionally got out of control. For example, Manson alternately shouted, then abruptly be-

came quiet, as he menacingly made a noose out of the microphone cable. At other times, he'd pace up and down, change
the subject, and mutter to himself.

Each time the crew stopped to change a tape, Manson asked
me how he was doing, as if he needed my approval. It later
occurred to me that even in this highly bizarre situation, where
logical thought was largely irrelevant, the instinctive relationship set up by the first seven seconds made a difference.

Research shows that we start to make up our minds about
other people within seven seconds of first meeting them. Much
of this is unspoken, as my first few seconds were with Charles
Manson. But we are communicating with our eyes, faces, bodies, and attitudes.

Consciously or unconsciously, we're signaling to other people what our true feelings are and what we really want to
happen in an encounter. It's almost a reflex action, like the
pupil of an eye reacting to light. People, in the presence of
others, affect each other's bodies. Sometimes imperceptibly,
sometimes noticeably, we influence each other's breathing,
heart rate, skin temperature, sweat glands, blood pressure, eye
blinks, body motions—even the way some tiny hairs stand up
on the skin. In the first seven seconds, we also trigger in each
other a chain of emotional reactions, ranging from reassurance
to fear.

FIRST IMPRESSIONS

Stop and think about some of the most memorable meetings
you've had with other people. It may have been an introduction
to a friend or a lover. It may have been a job interview. It may
have been a rude shock—an intruder, a stranger, someone very
unwelcome. Or it might have been pleasant—a surprise party.
Whatever it was, try to focus on the first seven seconds of the
encounter. What did you feel and think? How did you "read"
the other people and how do you think they read you? How
accurate or lasting were the first impressions on both sides? Did

the tone in the opening seven seconds carry over to the rest of the meeting? Was the ice broken initially, or was tension established?

Now, review the last few days. Did you meet anyone new? Try to remember. What happened in the first seven seconds? What was directly or indirectly communicated in that time? How did you *feel* about this person?

Finally, think about yourself. What sort of impression do you believe you make on others in the first seven seconds? How aware are you of all the verbal and nonverbal signals you send to others as you come face-to-face, or even when you speak to others over the telephone? How aware are you of the underlying messages sent by eyes, face, voice, and body (yours and others')? How much control do you feel you have over these variables? It's important to focus on these questions because they help define not just your communications skills in the abstract but also who you are and how others perceive you.

Try to read other people's nonverbal signals in every situation. It may be business or personal, at a convention or an intimate dinner. It's amazing how accurate these messages are. We all send them out and we all receive them.

Some body language specialists suggest that you can interpret someone's hidden agenda from the positioning of arms, legs, torso, and so forth. That's partially true. But it's not so simple. You also have to take into account the other person's pitch, tone, rate of speech, phrasing, breathing—even eye dilation. The interpretation has to be a blend of literal observation and instinct. For example, some people would interpret folded arms to signal a defensive attitude when, in fact, there are people who actually fold their arms for comfort. One signal alone can be misleading. Learn to look at and listen to the "composite" person.

Most children are natural at reading others. They know when to ask Daddy or Mommy for something. They know when to keep quiet and leave the room. They know when there's tension between their parents. And they know when everyone thinks they're adorable. As we get older, we begin to block these natural absorbing techniques. We need to open them up again. Pay attention. Watch. Listen. Talk less. Notice whether people's *words* are saying the same things as their *vocal tones*.

EASY MONEY

I recall producing a documentary on gangs for WCBS–TV in New York. We interviewed a group of tough teenagers between the ages of fifteen and eighteen who were in a halfway house being rehabilitated. These young criminals robbed people on the subways. On a "good" day, they claimed, they made three hundred to four hundred dollars in cash without ever being detected by the police or turned in by their victims. We were having our initial meeting with these youngsters. They agreed to take us later on a tour of the subways and show us how they performed their "work."

As they entered the conference room, it was clear that if any of them asked you for your money, you'd probably turn it over. The leader of the group was Henry, a seventeen-year-old who exhibited a great deal of confidence. I asked Henry why he robbed people.

"Because crime pays, man!"

"What do you mean?"

"I make fifteen hundred dollars a week in cash in the subways. I don't have to hurt nobody. If somebody don't give me their money, I go to somebody else. I don't want flack, man. I don't want problems. I don't want to draw attention. I been doin' it for three years. Now, tell me, where can I get me a job makin' fifteen hundred dollars a week?"

"Why are you in the rehabilitation program?"

"I ain't sure I'm gonna stay. They talked me into tryin' so they could teach me a job skill. I'm open to listenin'. But I ain't positive I'll never go back out on the streets again."

That was not a comforting thought. We asked for a demonstration of how the gang members "rolled" their victims. I asked Henry, in particular, how he picked victims. He told me he looked for people shuffling along, heads down, eyes averted, isolated, and frightened when they saw him. In effect, he used his senses and his instincts to read their body language.

I looked around the room, picked out individuals, and asked Henry if they would make good victims. He said yes or no.

"Would I make a good victim?" I asked.

"No, I wouldn't mess with you."

"Why not?"

"When I firs' walked into th' room, you stood up and turned right toward me. Your eyes looked right into my eyes and then you looked me up and down from head to toe as if measurin' me, to judge if you could take me in a fight if you had to. Those kinda people cause trouble. I might hafta kill you to get your money. I wouldn't want t' hafta do that. Not for your sake, but for mine."

This relatively uneducated street tough could instinctively read the body language that would allow him to make a hit and be successful. He made that determination in less than seven seconds.

COMMUNICATE OR DIE

Captain Eugene "Red" McDaniel was a Navy pilot shot down in North Vietnam and held as a prisoner of war for six years. In his book *Scars and Stripes,* he describes the desperate need of prisoners to communicate with one another to maintain morale. He says POWs tended to die much sooner if they couldn't communicate. On many occasions, Captain McDaniel endured torture rather than give up his attempts to stay in touch with other prisoners, especially when he was in solitary confinement. Prisoners risked death to work out a complicated communications system where they would write under plates, cough, sing, tap on walls, laugh, scratch, or flap laundry a certain number of times to transmit a letter of the alphabet.

Captain McDaniel writes, "One thing I knew, I had to have communications with my own people here in this camp. There were people like myself who wanted to live through this, if at all possible. Communication with each other was what the North Vietnamese captors took the greatest pains to prevent. They knew, as well as I and the others did, that a man could stand more pain if he is linked with others of his own kind in that suffering. The lone, isolated being becomes weak, vulnerable. I knew I had to make contact, no matter what the cost."[1] For those brave men, it was communicate or die.

When we think of survival, we usually list food, shelter, and clothing as the essentials. I believe communications belongs in that grouping. Babies have died in hospitals because of lack of attention, caring, and handling. Human communication is incredibly important, but most of us take it for granted and think we know how to do it. We've been told many times that we only use a tiny part of our brain. We use only a tiny part of our communications abilities as well. For example, how many facial expressions can you read?

FACE VALUE

Research shows that the eighty muscles of the face are capable of making more than seven thousand different facial expressions.[2] Most of us can read if someone is happy or sad or frightened, but what about the other nuances? Develop a curiosity about what you see in other people's faces. Do you see apprehension, shyness, curiosity, hostility, humor, warmth? As you get better and better at reading these signals, you will become much more successful at interpersonal communications.

Facial expression is often the most difficult area of nonverbal communication to master because we are taught early that our faces can give us away. Many people, particularly business executives, freeze their faces regardless of the emotional state they are in. They believe a poker face is a strategic advantage. Sometimes it is. But often, you only gain complete credibility with an audience when they feel you're completely open and not masking anything from them. The viewer generally perceives the warmer, more vulnerable personality as being stronger and less afraid.

MIRROR IMAGE

Let's try something you've probably never done before. Look in a mirror and study your own face. Begin to talk about a political issue and see which part of your face moves and which doesn't. Using the same subject matter, repeat the conversation; however, imagine that now you're speaking to a child. See if your face softens and if your eyes become more expressive, and if there is a tendency to care more that the listener understands what you are saying. Most people do tend to use more facial expression when talking to children.

Still looking in the mirror, think of something funny until you smile. When you do, see if your eyes smile as well as your mouth. It's important not to try to make a smile but to concentrate until an incident or something someone said comes to mind which causes the reaction naturally. Dwell on that thought until your whole face smiles, including your eyes. Note carefully *how* your face smiles.

LISTEN UP

Concentrate on listening and reacting. As you listen to a newscast, allow yourself the freedom of relaxing completely and then, as if your face were your only means of communication, try to transmit the feeling of that story to an imaginary third party by use of your face only. Do the same exercise in a mirror, imagining different stories and trying to transmit your feelings about them.

Think of a very happy time in your life, a very sad time, and a time when you were most angry; think of a time when you were frightened or concerned and try to show all these emotions as if you were a mute. Study very carefully how your face moves and concentrate on how it feels so that when you aren't looking in a mirror, you can re-create that look simply by muscle tension and feeling.

Ask a question such as "Did you enjoy the concert last night?" and see if your face can show an inquisitive characteristic. "Do you really mean that?" "Is it time to go?" Try thinking those sentences without speaking and somehow get the meaning across using only your face.

THE MASK

Even if you're not a fan of television, turn on your set and watch it carefully for half an hour. Alternately turn the sound off and on. Change channels frequently and watch the facial expressions of the actors and actresses. Also watch their reaction shots, when they're not speaking lines. Angela Lansbury, star of "Murder, She Wrote," is famous for her reaction shots. See if you can interpret their meaning and then imitate the expressions.

We all wear masks, but it's necessary to drop the mask to communicate fully. Get used to using your face every time you speak.

Often, writers describe eyes as steely, knowing, mocking, piercing, glowing, and so on, or they may refer to a burning, cold, or hurt glance. Look in a mirror. Can you demonstrate any of these emotional states just by using your eyes?

The duration of a stare, opening the eyelids, squinting, or the dozens of other manipulations of skin and eyes can send out many meanings. The most important thing to consider is the feeling behind the look or the stare. This tends to give the object being stared at either human or nonhuman status. Have you ever had a person stare at you as if you were an object and not a person? It's chilling, isn't it? If we wish to ignore someone pointedly and treat him with contempt, we give him the same unfocused look as if we didn't really see him. Panhandlers are often treated this way.

To acknowledge humanness, we avoid the blank stare and

focus our eyes while relaxing our faces. This creates a warmth and empathy with another person. There are a variety of ways to avoid a blank look—for example, the sideways glance, the furtive glance, the lidded look, the surprised expression which says, "Oh, how nice to see you," and so forth.

Basically, we're dealing with the art of conversation, encouraging others to speak by reacting facially as we listen to what they say. This is called active listening. Speaking with enthusiasm when it's our turn is also essential to good conversation.

CONVERSATIONALLY SPEAKING

Good communication starts with good conversation. If you converse well, then you should be able to transfer that ability to a lectern or TV or any other format.

To gauge your conversational skills, you need constructively critical feedback from someone else. Ask a spouse, friend, or coworker to candidly appraise your conversational skills, based on these criteria:

• Are you self-centered or other-oriented? Do you try to dominate conversations? Do you talk too much, overexplain, or lecture others? Are you a complainer? Or do you draw other people out on topics they're clearly interested in discussing? Are you a sympathetic listener? Do you smile, laugh easily, and respond to others genuinely?

• Do you have interesting things to say? Can you discuss subjects besides your job or home life? Do you occasionally use colorful language? Do you avoid trite expressions?

• Are you lively or dull? Do you speak in a monotone and without enthusiasm? Do you get to the point quickly and engagingly or do you belabor points? Are you passive and nonresponsive or active in the give-and-take of conversation?

• Do you encourage monologues or dialogues? Do you ask others open-ended questions that draw them out? Or are your questions "closed," prompting just one-word responses? Open-ended questions often begin with "how" or "what"; they elicit detail. You may need to use closed questions occasionally, as in this series of questions. You can recognize closed questions because they often begin with "do you . . ."

• Do you pontificate or do you ask others how *they* feel about a subject? Are you open, candid, direct, and friendly, or tight-lipped, secretive, elliptical, and aloof?

Ask yourself the question I ask every client: If you could improve a single thing about the way you communicate, what would it be?

THE TEN MOST COMMON PROBLEMS

Here are the ten most common problems in communications. Read the list. If any of them apply to you, the principles in this book will help you solve them.

1. Lack of initial rapport with listeners
2. Stiffness or woodenness in use of body
3. Presentation of material is intellectually oriented; speaker forgets to involve the audience emotionally
4. Speaker seems uncomfortable because of fear of failure
5. Poor use of eye contact and facial expression
6. Lack of humor
7. Speech direction and intent unclear due to improper preparation
8. Inability to use silence for impact
9. Lack of energy, causing inappropriate pitch pattern, speech rate, and volume
10. Use of boring language and lack of interesting material

Various polls show that the ability to communicate well is ranked the number-one key to success by leaders in business, politics, and the professions. If you don't communicate effectively, you may not die, like some POWs or neglected babies we mentioned earlier, but you also won't live as fully as you should, nor will you achieve personal goals. This was a lesson drummed into me at a very early age.

BOYHOOD LESSONS

I grew up in the little factory town of Warren, Ohio. My father was a foreman at the local Packard Electric plant, which made wiring for GM cars. Dad had a high school diploma, which was as far as anyone in our family had ever gone in school. But he had a lot of common sense.

He taught me a fundamental lesson about communicating that relates to the idea of "absorbing" other people before you "project" yourself. He said, "Boy, you can't learn anything when you're talkin'." (I later heard that advice expressed as "God gave you two ears and one mouth so you could listen twice as much as you speak.") Based on what Dad told me, I tried to listen to other people and observe them before I spoke up. That was the era of the belief that "children should be seen and not heard." Learning to listen made me more sensitive to other people, perhaps too sensitive, when I first ventured out into the business world.

I was all of ten years old. The Korean War was on and my family was nearly broke, even though Dad was working hard. My mother used to embroider handkerchiefs, and I would take them out and sell them door-to-door. I was terrible at it. I would always read the expressions on the faces of my potential customers and realize they couldn't afford to buy. I began to recognize disappointment, hesitation, even embarrassment in my customers' faces. Often they didn't need to say a word. I felt sorry for them, so frequently I'd sell a handkerchief for less than it was worth. My mother was no fool. She made me stop selling the handkerchiefs, and my brother assumed all the sales duties. Even at age ten, I was reading things in people's faces. And while it made me the worst handkerchief salesman in Warren, Ohio, it would serve me well later in life, especially in my career.

FROM HANDKERCHIEFS TO HOLLYWOOD STARS

Television and I grew up together. The first time I saw it was in 1949. I was nine years old. On the tiny screen was a test pattern with Howdy Doody's picture. I don't remember watching much television again until I was fifteen or sixteen, when I went out of my way to see ball games, "The Jackie Gleason Show," and "Toast of the Town" with Ed Sullivan. As it did for millions of others, TV soon became a part of my life, but I had no idea it could be a career.

When I went off to Ohio University, the only way I could finance my education was with part-time jobs. There was an opening at the university radio station. I auditioned and was hired. I became the 7 A.M. sign-on disc jockey. Although I enjoyed being on the air, I was more excited by the scripting, the deadlines, the creativity, and the enthusiasm of the other students. Radio—and later TV—also gave me the opportunity to provide the link between audiences and significant events and personalities in politics, sports, business, and entertainment. For the next four years I was consumed by broadcasting.

I graduated from college in 1962. I had two job offers: one as a sports announcer at a radio station in Columbus; the other as a prop boy for a television station in Cleveland. The radio job paid more. But my intuition told me that the future was in television. So I became a prop boy, which is another word for gofer (as in "Go fer the coffee, kid").

The station was just starting a local television program called "The Mike Douglas Show." The goal was to create a show that could be syndicated nationally, which most people thought would be impossible from Cleveland, Ohio. The show's gimmick was that Mike, an almost unknown former band singer, would cohost each week with a different Hollywood star. It worked and the show became the most widely viewed nationally syndicated talk-variety show in television history up to that time. "The Mike Douglas Show" was eventually seen in 180 cities, lasted almost twenty years, and had more viewers at one point than NBC–TV's "The Tonight Show," with Johnny Carson. Most of the credit for the creation of this program goes to executive producer Woody Fraser, program manager Chet Collier, and a few talented others.

I was fortunate to join their group in the show's first few months and my career grew with the show. By working very hard, I was promoted to assistant director, which is a gofer with stripes. I wrote cue cards for the songs, I ran for sandwiches for the stars, I picked up guests at the airport and brought them to the studio. I did whatever anybody asked. It was a great learning experience. Suddenly I was working daily with the biggest stars of the time—people like Bob Hope, Pearl Bailey, Liberace, Jack Benny, and Judy Garland. I mention these names because it was from these and others that I learned the elements of effective communications. Each person I met had some impact on me. But the greatest impact of all was made by television itself.

2
TELEVISION CHANGED
THE RULES

Television is a controversial medium. Some people think it's good. Some don't. Much has been written about how TV has changed the way we view the world. What I've learned first-hand is that television has also changed the way we view each other. As a result of TV, people today expect to be made comfortable in every communications situation. When someone speaks to them, they want to relax and listen just as they do when a TV professional entertains them in their living room. So when you and I communicate, we are unconsciously judged by our audience against the standards set by David Letterman and Dan Rather. You may think that's unfair, but that's the way it is. You don't need to be as funny as Letterman or as confident as Rather. But you're expected to be at least as comfortable, knowledgeable, and to the point as any good guest on a television show. In our subconscious minds, the style that's acceptable on television—relaxed, informal, crisp, and enter-taining—has become the modern standard for an effective communicator.

QUICK-CUT COMMUNICATIONS

Today we're all tuned to receive information much more quickly, and we get bored in a hurry if things slow down. The video age has sped up our cognitive powers. We get to the point faster. Because we've become accustomed to video editing, our minds skip ahead. When I started in television, programs had longer segments than they have today. Videotape and its editing process have tightened up not only television but the way we communicate. This has contributed significantly to making us a more impatient society. We're often too glib when we shouldn't be. That's why sometimes changing your rate of speech, your movements, or how quickly you get to the point can help you gain control of a situation. People who watch the evening news see entire South American cities collapse under earthquakes in sixty seconds or less. So if you're just talking for sixty seconds, you'd better be good *and* interesting.

SEE IT AND SAY IT

Images help. If you can see a picture in your mind and describe it, others will stay tuned in. For example, a number of my clients are chief financial officers (CFOs) of large corporations. The truth is, when one CFO speaks to a group of other CFOs, the material is not exactly "Saturday Night Live" in style. That's not a criticism of the speakers. It's just that there's a lot of statistical data that have to be used in any financial presentation. We're stuck with it. The trick is—whenever possible—to go beyond the deadly abstraction of numbers and relate what you have to say in a way that brings the numbers to life.

Businesspeople can be remarkably adept at expressing technical ideas in a creative way. Look at the language describing corporate takeovers these days. Terms like "poison pills," "white knights," and "shark repellent" put life into discussions of highly technical business maneuvers.

There are many interesting ways to communicate facts and statistics. For instance, if speakers can paint word pictures, as opposed to just using words, or can use emotionally charged, intriguing words, they'll be more interesting. If you're talking about imported oil, for example, instead of just quoting how many tons of oil come into a country every day or every year, you might say, "That's enough to fill every football stadium in this country ten times over."

WANTED: ALIVE, NOT DEAD

Whether you're a lawyer presenting a case to a jury or a businessperson making a presentation of some kind, the techniques of television apply to what you're doing, in terms of brevity, quick cut, pacing, visual reinforcements, and colorful language. We're in a headline society now and we need to realize this, whether we think it's a good thing or not. In today's society, long-winded people will soon be as extinct as the dinosaur. You have to be punchy and graphic in your conversation—at least some of the time—to hold people's interest.

Here are some quotes. To the left of each quote I've composed a deadly version of a lively thought.

Dull	*Interesting*
The two leading ways to achieve success are improving upon existing technology and finding a means of evading a larger obligation.	The two leading recipes for success are building a better mousetrap and finding a bigger loophole. *—Edgar A. Schoaff*
To construct an amalgam, you have to be willing to split open its component parts.	To make an omelet, you have to be willing to break a few eggs. *—Robert Penn Warren*
Capital will not produce great pleasure, but it will remunerate a large research staff to examine the questions proposed for a solution.	Money won't buy happiness, but it will pay the salaries of a large research staff to study the problem. *—Bill Vaughan*

In this video age we're all broadcasters. We transmit our own programs. We receive ratings from our audiences. We've been absorbed by the medium of television and now *we* are part of that medium. We can project comedy, drama, information, or news. We can write the scripts and deliver the parts. And we can move an audience to laughter, tears, or boredom. Marshall McLuhan said, "The medium is the message." I believe each person is his own message, whatever medium he chooses.

3
YOU ARE THE MESSAGE

The most pressure-packed communications spotlight in the world follows the president of the United States, and on the morning of Monday, October 8, 1984, the pressure on Ronald Reagan was particularly intense.

The press had pretty much decided that Walter Mondale had won the first television debate with Reagan in Louisville the night before. Speculation swept the country that there was hope for Mondale yet, and that maybe, just maybe, he could pull the election out over the popular seventy-three-year-old president, who had appeared so tired and confused to the nation's viewers.

A couple of days later, I received a call from the White House. Up to that point, I had played a small, creative consulting role on the president's Tuesday Team, the group masterminding the reelection campaign. Now some of the president's staff wanted me to come down to Washington and see what I could do about averting a second TV debate disaster, an event even *they* feared could cost Ronald Reagan the election. There was great resistance to bringing me in, because many people felt that the president had been overcoached for the first debate. Nancy Reagan was upset that the president had performed so badly against Mondale after all that coaching, and since she didn't know me, she probably thought, "God, that's all we need—one more consultant. We had too many the first time." She wasn't wrong, but my aim was to provide the structure needed to bring the president back to basics.

THE REASSURANCE ISSUE

What the American people wanted from the president, I felt, was some reassurance that he wasn't too old for the job, and given that, they would reelect him. Clearly, they hadn't received that reassurance in the first debate, although his supposed losses from that performance were exaggerated. Although there had been a drop in Reagan's polling results in the large cities of the Northeast—which were not his natural constituency anyway—I was told his numbers stayed even or actually went up in places like Texas after the first debate. Nevertheless, it *was* important for the president to do well in the second debate.

When I arrived at the White House, the first thing Reagan's top aides, Jim Baker and Michael Deaver, told me was that I would not be talking to Mr. Reagan directly. They said, "We'd like your ideas, and if we think they're good, we'll present them to the president." So I said fine, and we got down to business.

DEFINING GOALS

"What are the president's goals for the second debate?" I asked. Their replies were vague, so I went through a checklist of possible objectives.

Finally Baker said, "Maybe you ought to go to the debate practice this afternoon. Don't say anything, just sit in the back and watch, and give us your observations."

At 4 P.M., I arrived at the little theater in the Executive Office Building next to the White House. There were two lecterns on the stage, with Reagan standing at one and his budget director, David Stockman, at the other. Several members of the administration were set up as a panel of questioners. The moment I walked in, I could see that the president was uncomfortable, out of sorts, and tired. He clearly didn't want to be there, but this mock debate was on his schedule.

STOCKMAN'S *OTHER* BOOK

Someone fired a question at Stockman and he gave a perfect answer, reading it out of some notebook put together by Ph.D.s. In response, the president ad-libbed, fumbling around a bit. Then back to Stockman, who read a perfect rebuttal and buried the president again, making him look confused about the facts. Every time they finished a round, somebody in the audience would raise a hand and say, "Mr. President, the tonnage on that warhead is wrong. The date of that treaty was so-and-so," and they'd correct him.

I watched this performance for about twenty minutes, with Stockman's written answers annihilating the president, and Reagan trying to remember all the detailed facts and statistics as he had in the first debate. I signaled for Deaver and Baker to come out into the hall. "If you think he was bad in Kentucky, wait till he gets to Kansas City. It'll be a disaster if you keep this up."

"Well, what do we do?" they asked.

ACCESS TO THE PRESIDENT

I told them to cancel the mock debates, get everyone off his back, and give me access to him for a couple of hours between then and Sunday, when the second debate was scheduled. I also asked for the last half hour before the debate alone with the president. "If you give me that," I told them, "he'll win. If you don't, he'll probably lose." I realized that sounded presumptuous, but actually I was gambling on Reagan and his innate gift of communication. I felt pretty sure that if I could get him back to being *himself* again, he'd be okay.

When I went back into the theater, they were still at it, correcting everything the president said. Finally, someone asked him a fairly tough question, and he gave a brilliant answer.

There was complete silence. So I stood up in the back and called out, "Mr. President, that was a terrific answer!" Reagan flashed me a big smile and seemed to grow about four inches. He was like a guy in a batting slump who finally puts one over the wall. He really needed someone to give him a cheer.

Two days later, I met with Reagan and his aides. Again I asked the question. "Mr. President, what's your goal in the second debate?"

He obviously hadn't thought much about it, and finally he said, "Well, Mondale's saying some things that aren't true and I've got to correct the record."

LET REAGAN BE REAGAN

"Mr. President," I said, "there are five strategies you can choose from. You can attack, defend, counterattack, sell, or ignore. You've picked defense, which is the weakest possible position. If you do that, you'll lose again." That got his attention. Then I talked to him about communications, debates, and what I thought the public expected. I said, "You didn't get elected on details. You got elected on themes. Every time a question is asked, relate it to one of your themes. You know enough facts, and it's too late to learn new ones now, anyway."

After about fifteen minutes of conversation, Mike Deaver, the man who knew the president best, slipped me a note that said, "He's really tuned in. Keep going!"

THE PEPPER DRILL

After that, we did what I call a pepper drill. We fired questions at the president and he had about ninety seconds for each answer, which was considerably less time than he would have in the actual debate.

"What I want you to do, Mr. President, is to go back to your instincts. Just say what comes to you out of your experience."

I asked others in the room not to interrupt the drill but to make a note of anything they thought should be corrected later.

That was a little risky because there were a lot of high-powered people there, but I knew that I was in charge and that I had to remain in charge of that session until the president regained his rhythm and confidence.

For the next hour, we fired away at him. Every time he'd start to stumble, I'd ask, "What do your instincts tell you about this?" and he'd come right back on track. He was very good. Finally I said, "Mr. President, if you do that Sunday night, you're home free."

THE UNMENTIONABLE TOPIC

On Saturday, I met with Mike Deaver in his office prior to my ninety-minute meeting with the president in the White House residential quarters. Before we went upstairs, Deaver warned me, "Don't introduce anything new at this meeting. Let's just see if the president has any questions or concerns about the debate, and if he has, we'll go over them."

I said, "I have two concerns. One, the close that the president has prepared is too long. It won't fit in the time allotted."

"It's too late to change it," Deaver said. "The president's working on it. He's got it."

I offered a second close, which was much shorter. Deaver rejected it. Then I asked, "Has anybody talked to the president about the age issue?"

Deaver replied, "We don't want to introduce anything new."

I took that to mean that they'd already discussed it, that it was none of my business, and that they didn't want me to get into that sensitive area with the president.

On the way to the president's residence, Deaver and I met up with Robert McFarlane, who was then national security advisor, and we all went upstairs to join the president. He came in carrying his yellow pad and looking relaxed in casual slacks, loafers, and a polo shirt.

The four of us discussed several issues and the president read through his closing statement. Then, as we were walking out toward the security elevator, I realized that no one had discussed the age question. Although I had been warned not to bring up anything new, I was sure some reporter would ask the question. So I said, "Mr. President, what are you going to do when they say you're too old for the job?"

He stopped cold and blinked. Silence.

"It's critical that you get by that issue successfully," I said.

He thought for a moment. Then he smiled and said, "Well, there's an old line I've used before about . . ." and he told me what he planned to say.

"Fine," I said. "That's a good answer. But whatever happens, say that and nothing else. Don't get drawn into the age question at all. Just say your line and stand there."

"I got it," he said. We left.

On Sunday, in Kansas City, I met with the president in his hotel suite just before the debate. He led me into a back bedroom where there was one chair and a bed. I expected him to take the chair, but he took off his jacket, bounced up on the bed, and said, "Okay, coach, what do we do?"

We ran through the strategy one more time—how to go on offense, when to move, what to hit on. He had it down pretty well. Then I gave him a pep talk and asked him if he was ready.

"Let's go get 'em," he said.

ONE FOR THE GIPPER

During the debate, I sat in a room under the stage watching the monitor. Sure enough, someone asked the age question. Everybody around me groaned. "Don't worry," I said. "Here comes a home run." Up on stage, Reagan was saying that, of course, he felt up to the job, and then he let Mondale have it: ". . . and I want you to know that I will not make age an issue of this campaign. I am not going to exploit for political purposes my opponent's youth and inexperience." It was not just the president's words. It was his timing, inflection, facial expression, and body language which made the moment powerful.

As far as I was concerned, the debate was over. The news media had their lead quote for the next day, and everybody had a laugh. I watched Mondale's face. Even he broke into a smile, but I could see in his eyes that he knew it was over, too. I could almost hear him thinking, "Son of a gun, the old man got away with it! He got a laugh on that line, and I can't top it." The public had the reassurance they were looking for, and Reagan had the election won.

THE COMPOSITE YOU

This story wraps up everything I've ever learned about successful communication. It says, *"You are the message."* What does that mean, exactly? It means that when you communicate with someone, it's not just the words you choose to send to the other person that make up the message. You're also sending signals about what kind of person *you* are—by your eyes, your facial expression, your body movement, your vocal pitch, tone, volume, and intensity, your commitment to your message, your sense of humor, and many other factors.

The receiving person is bombarded with symbols and signals from you. Everything you do in relation to other people causes them to make judgments about what you stand for and what your message is. *"You are the message"* comes down to the fact that unless you identify yourself as a walking, talking message, you miss that critical point.

The words themselves are meaningless unless the rest of you is in synchronization. The total you affects how others feel about you and respond to you. In the case of the Reagan-Mondale debate, the audience really had just one thing on its mind: Is the president too old to serve another term? Reagan was very popular with the majority of voters. But was he physically capable of handling a second presidential term? The president could have insisted in words that he was feeling fit and able. And he certainly did that. But that was only a small part of the message.

In the first debate, the president had seemed tired and nervous and even confused at times. He now needed to demonstrate that he was still the same Ronald Reagan the voters had elected in 1980. My role in coaching him was to remind him that his objective in the debates was to communicate that composite personality which the voters liked so much. My advice to the president was simple: "You are the message."

ARE YOU A WINNER?

What does all this mean to you in terms of getting what you want by being who you are? What it means is that your composite message determines whether you're going to be successful in whatever career you've chosen, whether you're going to move up in the management of your company, whether you're going to be a winner or a loser, whether you're going to succeed in negotiating situations, whether you're going to become a superstar or just another droning voice who eventually gets a wristwatch at retirement. The stakes are that high. It's that important for you to accept that *you* (the whole you) are the message—and that message determines whether or not you'll get what you want in this life.

Over the past twenty-five years, I've worked with literally thousands of business and political leaders, show business personalities, and men and women who just want to be successful. I've helped many of them learn to communicate more effectively, control communication environments, make persuasive presentations, field hostile questions from journalists or irate corporate shareholders, and generally handle the ever-changing communication situations we all find ourselves in every day. The secret of that training has always been *"You are the message."* If you are uncomfortable with who you are, it will make others uncomfortable, too. But if you can identify and use your good qualities as a person, others will want to be with you and cooperate with you.

A PERSONAL INVENTORY

Take a piece of paper and list personal assets that help you communicate. Consider your physical appearance, energy, rate of speech, pitch and tone of voice, animation and gestures, expressiveness of eyes, and ability to hold the interest of people who listen to you. Perhaps you can add other qualities. These assets form the best part of the composite you. Study the list to see which areas you wish to improve. Those categories you feel less confident of are also part of your total message. In this book, we'll show you, as the old song says, how to "accentuate the positive and eliminate the negative."

"You are the message" is a new way of looking at yourself and others. Sometimes we can make mistakes about others if, as we view them, we segment them and only get a partial picture. This person has good-looking hair; that person has no hair. This person should lose weight; that one should gain weight. We look at all these parts of people, but then we quickly perceive the person in totality. You can have the greatest head of hair in the world, or the greatest smile, or the greatest voice, or whatever, but after two minutes you're going to be looked at as a whole person. All of those impressions of your various parts will have been blended into one complete composite picture, and the other person will have a feeling about you based on that total impression. Enough of that image has to be working in your favor for you to be liked, accepted, and given what you want.

THE UNFORGETTABLE BENNETT

Bennett Cerf, former chairman of Random House Publishing, was a man who never gave in to the pressure of growing up completely. F ` was an incorrigible punster. He would make a joke about anything and always seemed to be in good humor. He had a tremendous interest in other people. This quality alone made him one of the most sought-after friends and hosts in the world. He wasn't great-looking, he didn't have a great voice, he wasn't even a great speaker, and yet he became well known on national television, where publishing house executives usually aren't public figures. The reason? People liked Bennett! They always had the feeling he cared about them and was interested in what they were doing—and he truly was. He was interested in everyone he met. After meeting Bennett and spending ten minutes with him, you would find yourself engrossed in a deep conversation about yourself. Bennett was probing, interested, caring. He never hesitated to offer advice or ideas. He never held back because he thought he might lose some of himself if he gave it to others.

I had enormous respect for Bennett. I only knew him well for a few months, but I knew him well enough to understand why people were drawn to him. At the most serious moments, the little boy in Bennett would surface, he would say something funny, and everyone would start to giggle. I've seen many other people who careened from crisis to crisis, but I always had the feeling that Bennett Cerf was laughing from crisis to crisis and enjoying the trip. Bennett Cerf built a publishing empire and was a successful businessman, yet he gave the overall impression that life was a lark.

MAKING SENSE OF YOUR SENSES

For the next week, whenever you meet someone, quickly form an overall impression. Do I like this person or not? Am I comfortable or not comfortable? As soon as the overall impression is formed, try to identify as many particulars as you can about the person. Look at eyes, face, attitude, style, and voice. This exercise will sharpen your instincts about people. It will enable you to better "read between the lines" with others. You'll quickly spot if people mean what they're saying. You'll more readily discern nuances from others—for example, if they're tired, depressed, bored, or anxious, or if their interest has suddenly been piqued (reading other people accurately is essential if you want to succeed in any sales or negotiating situation).

Practice by writing down everything your senses tell you about each person you meet. If you cannot list at least twelve impressions or observations, you need some concentrated work in this area. This exercise will sharpen your instincts about people.

The fact is, our senses are always working, although we've trained ourselves to ignore them at times by tuning out. The goal of opening up your senses and practicing this exercise is to expand the sensory radar that all of us have but that only the most astute communicators tap into. Have you ever noticed that some people—maybe a boss, a teacher, or a friend—seem to be able to read your mind at times? The gift some people have is that they have trained their sensory radar better than you have. You can become more like these master communicators by opening up your senses instead of shutting them down.

The fact that most of us only use a small percentage of our sensory potential is demonstrated by the heightened sensing abilities developed by certain handicapped people. For example, the blind often hear, touch, and smell with great perception and subtlety. It's not that their other senses are better or different than those of sighted people—they're just more acutely used.

THE MORNING SHOW

When I was in college, I cohosted an early morning radio program called "Yawn Patrol" with another student, Don Matthews. Don was a better broadcaster than I was. He had a terrific voice, a good sense of humor, and a natural radio style.

Don was blind. During our program, we sat close together at a table with a microphone hanging between us. Each day, Don made a list, in Braille, of the records he wanted to play for the following morning's show. My job was to read the news and to banter with him. If I was going to speak, I would cue Don by tapping his hand so that we wouldn't run over each other. We were extraordinarily successful together. Eventually we became so sensitized to each other's breathing and speech patterns that we were able to give up the "tap" system.

Because our show was the first broadcast of the day, I used to arrive about fifteen minutes before airtime, open up the radio station, and turn on the lights and the transmitter. That required throwing about three switches, then going to the control room, cueing up the national anthem, opening the microphones, and signing on the station. Once Don took his place at the table, we would start the show.

One morning, there was a power failure in town and my alarm clock didn't go off. I woke up with a start, jumped into my clothes, and raced to the station, knowing that I was late. As I arrived, I heard the national anthem playing. I went directly to the studio. Don was there and we went through the program. I assumed that someone else, perhaps an engineer, had shown up early and turned on the equipment.

After the program, I asked Don who had turned on the transmitter. He said, "I did."

I was stunned. "How could you have turned it on?"

Don explained, "I used to follow you around when you turned everything on in the morning, so I knew basically where everything was. But about a week ago, when we were in the transmitter room, I noticed that there was a slight breeze coming from the right side of the room, which told me that there had to be a window open. When I arrived at the studio and you weren't here, I realized you must have overslept. So I went around to the back of the building, lifted the iron grate to the bottom window, lowered myself to the sill, lifted the window, and got into the transmitter room. Once inside, it was pretty easy to find the buttons by feel, since I'd heard you snap them on every day." He chuckled and went on, "It didn't matter that it was dark. It's always dark to me. So I got to the control room. I knew where you kept the national anthem record, so I cued it up and decided to start the show myself."

He said it all matter-of-factly, but I realized how keen his senses had to be to go through a series of fairly complicated steps without having the gift of sight.

TEST YOUR SENSES

You can begin to heighten the powers of your senses right now. Close your eyes. Focus on listening as intently as you can. Even if you're in a quiet room, you may hear the hum of the fluorescent lights or the rustle of the trees outside—sounds you filtered out just a moment ago.

Next, focus on sight without sound. Look out the window at moving objects or at people and study them closely. If you're near a TV, turn it on without the sound and just watch. Try to mentally list five different characteristics of each object or person you observe.

Finally, close your eyes again and try to picture streets where you often walk. Either in your mind or on a piece of paper, catalog every building and landscaped area you can recall in the greatest possible detail. Later, walk those streets and make a note of anything you missed in your inventory. We often *look* at but fail to *observe* people, places, and things.

OBSERVE OR DIE

One of my clients was a combat infantry officer in Vietnam. He says that he survived the war, in part, because he realized the importance of keen observation. "I could walk into a thicket of jungle and tell you if someone—or something—had passed through recently. I'd look for freshly broken twigs and grass that hadn't sprung up again—things a casual passerby might never see.

"Today, as I walk city streets or ride subways, I'm aware of exits, blind spots, dead ends, and places of vulnerability—all sorts of things we were sensitive to in 'Nam. During my tour, I learned to speak a little Vietnamese. But even if I didn't understand each word, I could always read the person's face. Even today, I can spot in someone else the quickest flicker of fear, apprehension, anger, or hostility."

"DON'T CHANGE ME"

Many clients I work with come in and say, "I don't want you to change me." Well, I can't change anyone. All I can do is help them identify and bring out their best qualities, the ones that communicate a positive message. I'll often sit down with someone who's quite good at communicating on a one-to-one level—someone who's friendly, warm, and articulate. We'll have a good conversation. Then I'll turn on the video camera and ask the person to stand up at the lectern and answer a few questions. Suddenly, that person, who is basically a good communicator, changes into someone entirely different. He becomes self-conscious, wooden, dull, uninteresting, tongue-tied, and cold. That person has changed himself, and then my job becomes one of trying to get him to change back into that warm, comfortable person he was when we were just sitting and chatting.

So when I say that you can get what you want by being who you are, I mean that you don't have to make any dramatic changes in your personality. You don't have to assume a phony posture. You just have to be yourself at your best. The truth is you already have the magic of good communications within you, because nobody can play *you* as well as you can.

REMEMBER BACK

Take a piece of paper and list three times in your life when you know you've communicated successfully. Think about those times. What made them work? I'm sure of a few things: You were committed to what you were saying, you knew what you were talking about, and you were so wrapped up in the moment you lost all feelings of self-consciousness.

Another critical point: Once you reach a comfortable, successful level of communications, you *never* have to change it, no matter what the situation or circumstances or the size of the audience. I define an audience as anyone other than yourself.

Whether there's one person or a thousand people listening to you, or if you're on television and there are millions watching, the essential principles hold true. The key element is that you *not* change or adapt your essential "self" to different audiences or different media. The thing that most confuses people trying to learn to be good communicators is the idea that somehow they have to act differently when giving an after-dinner speech than they would while being interviewed on television or for a job, or while conducting a staff meeting. They think they have to act all these different ways, and nobody's given them the script to do this. Remember: *You are the message,* and once you can "play yourself" successfully, you'll never have to worry again.

IT'S ALWAYS A DIALOGUE

The trick in good communications is to be consistently *you,* at your best, in all situations. All communication is a dialogue. You (the speaker) are selecting and sending symbols (words, facial expressions, and so forth) to the audience. The audience may not be speaking back, but they're sending you symbols as well—for example, facial expressions and body language. Learn to read those symbols coming back to you.

THE GUEST METER

The best communicators I've ever known never changed their style of delivery from one situation to another. They're the same whether they're delivering a speech, having an intimate conversation, or being interviewed on a TV talk show.

During the late 1960s, as executive producer of the Mike Douglas television talk show, I would decide who the program's guests would be and how much airtime each guest should receive. Gradually, my ear became trained to listen for the interesting stories, the easy conversationalists, and the hesitations ("No, I don't want to talk about that"). I was able to tune in to the rhythm of their voices. Sometimes I'd only have a five-minute conversation from an airport telephone booth and have to decide, right then and there, how good a guest would be, what kind of an impression he or she would make on the TV audience, and how much airtime to allow. I developed an internal "guest meter." Sometimes I was fooled, of course, but most of the time my first impression of the message the person was presenting—even over the telephone—turned out to be a pretty accurate gauge of that guest's impact.

Stop and think for a minute. If you were a TV producer, would you book yourself as a guest?

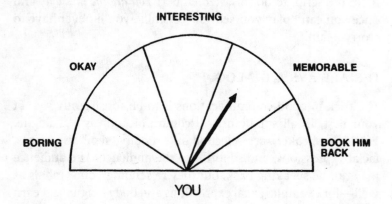

I also had the opportunity to see many of these excellent TV communicators perform in other situations, like after-dinner speaking. It really impressed me how they kept the same personal style and delivery they used on television. They didn't change a thing. Interestingly enough, Mike Douglas was not a particularly good after-dinner speaker, even though he was terrific as a TV talk show host. Whenever I heard him speak, I used to think, "Mike, if you'd just do up there at the podium what you do on the air, which is to have a good conversation, you'd be great at the lectern, too." So the principle here is not to change yourself because the environment changes, but rather to become totally comfortable with yourself wherever you are. Once you realize that *you* are the message, you can transmit that message to anyone anytime and be pretty successful at it.

THE GOOD NEWS

Now that I've told you what your goal should be, let me give you the good news. You can become as good as some of the people you admire on TV. And assessing your skills can be fun, because it helps you to know yourself better. It also improves your relationships with the people around you. In short, it helps you get what you want.

One important note: You can't rely on other people to change themselves to accommodate you. That's a strategy of reaction. The way to influence others is to do it actively—with your composite message. If there is a misunderstanding between the communicator (you) and the "communicatee" (your audience), it's the communicator's fault. This requires that *you* take complete responsibility for the flow of communications, whether you're speaking or listening. This is good news, because it empowers you to be, in effect, in charge of every communications situation you're in. You *can* change the mood and the flow of the communications exchange.

HOPELESS?

Bob Hope taught me that lesson when I was a young, twenty-three-year-old associate producer of "The Mike Douglas Show." I unexpectedly met Hope when he was on a media tour to promote his book *I Owe Russia Twelve Hundred Dollars.* I say "unexpectedly" because Hope was passing through Cleveland, Ohio, where our then local show was produced, when his publicist suddenly called us to say that the great comedian would appear on our program. In the sort of chance that can make or break a young person's career, all the producers senior to me were either ill or out of town on business when we got the chance to have Bob Hope as our star guest. I was so inexperienced that I thought management would cancel the show rather than let me take charge, but they gambled on me.

Hope arrived at the front door of the television station with a large entourage of public relations people, local friends, and hangers-on. I was pretty intimidated. I knew that Bob Hope's appearance could be the critical showpiece performance to help catapult "The Mike Douglas Show" into national syndication. As I met Hope, I mumbled nearly incoherently in trying to explain the show to him. Many of the people hanging around

Hope were rolling their eyes as if to say, "Who is this kid and what are we doing here?"

I was too scared to say so, but I really wanted Hope to stay for our entire ninety-minute show and sing, dance, and joke around. He wanted to plug his book and leave in five minutes. In the middle of my stammering, Hope grabbed my shoulders and steered me away from the others, through a doorway and into the scenery shop of the television station. Suddenly Bob Hope and I were alone.

He looked at me and said, "Kid, I know nothing about your show. I've never been on it and I don't know what you expect me to do. It's very important for you to speak up and tell people exactly what you want. I'm a big enough star to refuse whatever you request, if I decide to. But if I don't even know what you want, there's no way I can give it to you. Now, tell a little bit about the program and the host, when I'm on, where I enter, and what's expected of me."

I realized in a flash that I had one chance and had better go for it. I admitted to Hope that I was not the producer but that an awful lot depended on his staying for the entire program, to entertain as well as to plug his book.

He started to laugh and said, "The network is paying me a hundred thousand dollars to do that." He patted me on the shoulder and said, "Okay, now that I know what you want, I'll let you know what I'll do later. Let's see how it goes. In the meantime, just tell me when and where I go on."

As it turned out, Bob Hope stayed for the entire show. Once he was in front of the audience his natural performer instincts took over. He enjoyed Mike, they sang a duet, Bob danced and joked with the audience. His command performance undoubtedly helped "The Mike Douglas Show" later to be sold into national syndication.

After the show, as he was leaving, he saw me and said, "How'd I do, kid?"

"You were great, Mr. Hope."

He turned and pointed at me. "Next time, speak up." He smiled and left.

I never forgot that lesson—and I've never been afraid to speak to anyone since then. It's your responsibility—not your listener's—to insure that your message gets through, and if you don't speak up, people can't help you get what you want.

Let me demonstrate with one simple example. If you say to me, "I'll never lie to you," but you're looking at the floor when you say it, I could doubt that message or at least wonder, "Why doesn't he look at me when he says that? Maybe he's not telling the truth."

On the other hand, if you take charge and look me in the eye, the statement becomes not only believable but also reassuring, strong, and positive.

HAPPY TO BE HERE?

The words you choose to speak are important, but they're just part of your message. However, many people think that their words are the whole message. Corporate executives are famous for this. They often get up and send all sorts of weird signals to their audience. My favorite is "Ladies and gentlemen, I'm very happy to be here." But they're looking at their shoes as they say it. They have no enthusiasm whatsoever. They look either angry, frightened, or depressed about being there.

In fact, they're often only reading these words. So while the words say "happy to be here," the rest of the person is sending a very different message. The signals are confusing, and the audience will always go with the visual signals over the verbal ones. They'll say to themselves unconsciously, "He's telling me he's happy to be here, but he's really not. Therefore, he's either uncomfortable or a liar, or both." The speaker is the message and the message is negative.

SPEECH-READING TIPS

I once heard a story, which is probably apocryphal, about an executive invited to address a very distinguished audience at the Harvard Club. The night of the speech, the executive went to the platform carrying a long, erudite text written by his Ph.D. speechwriter. As he prepared to launch into reading the scholarly but dull remarks, he suddenly changed his mind, stopped, and looked up at the audience. He said, "You know, ladies and gentlemen, I pay a brilliant speechwriter a great deal of money to make sure that I sound intelligent, don't make any mistakes, and never utter an expletive." Then he smiled and added, "Well, the hell with that. I'm just going to talk with you tonight from the heart." He threw the speech aside, delivered his remarks extemporaneously, and got a standing ovation.

Of course, there may be times when you *must* read a text. But the point is, when you can, extemporize, using an outline. That makes you appear to be more comfortable. However, if you must read, you can become very skilled at making yourself sound conversational. Never write "I'm very happy to be here" to open a speech. In fact, the only thing you should have at the top of the page is the word "Greeting" and the name of the group you're addressing, so that you can't blank out on that. Then you're forced to extemporize the opening.

Look at the audience when you speak, and speak with sincerity. Don't make sentences too long. Use short, punchy phrases so you can scan the paper with your eyes and look up and deliver the speech. Don't be afraid to pause between lines. Don't look down to read the final word of every line. Instead, quickly glance down to "scoop up" the last few words of a sentence. Pause. Look up and speak directly to the audience. Then pause again for a "beat" before you look down to scoop up your next phrase.

Take your time. Most people rush back into the text because they're afraid they'll lose their place. Their heads bob up and down like yo-yos. Use one index finger to guide you back to where you left off in the text. To repeat: *Go slowly.* Time gets distorted when you're in front of an audience, and you may think you have to rush more than is necessary. Pace your looking down and looking up so that your eyes are always *up* at the end of a sentence. To achieve that, feel free to take an extra beat to silently scoop up the final words of each sentence with your eyes before delivering them directly to the audience.

Try reading the following remarks in that manner. Note how the text has been laid out for easy "scoop reading" and delivery.

IT IS NOT THE CRITIC WHO COUNTS;
NOT THE MAN WHO POINTS OUT
HOW THE STRONG MAN STUMBLED,
OR WHERE THE DOER OF DEEDS
COULD HAVE DONE BETTER.

THE CREDIT BELONGS TO THE MAN
WHO IS ACTUALLY IN THE ARENA;

WHOSE FACE IS MARRED
BY DUST AND SWEAT AND BLOOD;
WHO STRIVES VALIANTLY;
WHO ERRS AND COMES SHORT
AGAIN AND AGAIN;

WHO KNOWS THE GREAT ENTHUSIASMS,
THE GREAT DEVOTIONS,
AND SPENDS HIMSELF IN A WORTHY CAUSE;

WHO AT BEST KNOWS IN THE END
THE TRIUMPH OF HIGH ACHIEVEMENT;
AND WHO AT THE WORST

IF HE FAILS,
AT LEAST FAILS WHILE DARING GREATLY;
SO THAT HIS PLACE SHALL NEVER BE
WITH THOSE COLD AND TIMID SOULS
WHO KNOW NEITHER VICTORY NOR DEFEAT.
                              —*Theodore Roosevelt*

Don't use stark white, shiny paper. If you deliver the speech in a room that has bright lights overhead, the page will reflect, making it difficult to see. Instead, use off-white, matte-finish, porous paper. Have the speech typed on the upper two thirds of the page, double-spaced between lines, and sextuple-spaced between paragraphs. With that spacing, there is less chance of losing your place, and your eyes are never forced to the bottom of the page, making you look too far down and away from the audience. This helps you maintain eye contact.

Depending on your eyesight, you may need to adjust the size of the type and the darkness of the print. Generally, a slightly blown-up typeface is easier to read. Large type sizes are available on most typewriters or word processors today. Have the speech typed in such a way that ideas or sentences end on a page (see our sample above). Try to limit a single thought to one or two lines so that your eyes can scan it easily. It's better to have more pages than to have the speech crowded together and difficult to read.

Be sure you number the pages in case they get out of order during a practice session. I once saw a man run from a trailer to an auditorium with a forty-page speech. The wind caught the pages and blew them all over the parking lot. The good news was that they found all the pages; the bad news was that he forgot to number them and he was due on stage at that moment.

Never flip the pages on the podium so that they're upside down. When you finish a page, just slide it to the side, face up. That way the audience does not become overly aware of all these pages flying; otherwise they might pay more attention to that distraction than to the speech itself.

Never rush the speech just to get it over with because you're reading. If it has no value and isn't worth reading, don't do it. If it does have value, read it slowly enough and with enough pauses that the audience can follow what you're saying.

Just like the beginning of the speech, the ending should be pretty well memorized so that you can deliver the last few lines while looking at the audience. Again, the same comfortable feeling used in all good communications should be used here. The audience knows you're reading and so do you. There's no need to try to hide it, nor is there a need to feel self-conscious about reading. If the speech is interesting, and you're comfortable and committed to what you're saying, the audience will go away feeling, "That was an interesting speaker," not just "That was an interesting speech."

4
INSTINCTS AND RULES

A few strong instincts and a few plain rules suffice us.
—*Ralph Waldo Emerson*

Many traditional how-to books advise you to stride into a room and forcefully take charge, purposefully invading others' space and asserting your personality in an attempt to dazzle and impress. These books say this gives you charisma. They offer formulas on how to mix and match the "right" clothes. They instruct you to greet others by using viselike "power handshakes." They tell you to rivet your eyes on the other person as if you were a hypnotist. They even tell you what to order for lunch. If you follow all this advice, not only will you drive everyone else crazy, you'll drive yourself crazy.

In this book, we'll show you why immediately projecting yourself when entering a room is a mistake. We'll discuss how best to analyze or "absorb" the moods, feelings, and hidden agendas of the other people in that room. Only then can you project appropriately for that situation.

The problem I've always had with the exclusive use of "how to speak" books was that as I read them, I wondered, "How am I ever going to remember all these helpful pointers when I stand up to speak or otherwise communicate with others?"

I quickly realized that what was needed was a new, more instinctive approach to communications. That's when I began to develop *You Are the Message*. The idea really came from observing so many good communicators in the early days of television, watching them perform before live audiences as well as before the camera. I realized that these communicators didn't change their style from private conversation to an appearance before a large audience. They simply increased their energy at times but otherwise stayed conversational in every format.

In the old days, we'd read a book and it would give a list of dos and don'ts like "Stand up straight. Use your arms. Know your subject. Don't sway back and forth. Use eye contact" and so on. But today we sit in front of a television set and watch great communicators in our homes. We absorb everything about what they do—how they move, how they look, their sense of humor, their attitudes. This is how people learn to communicate today. It's visual. It's intuitive. It's kinetic. It's watching, feeling, sensing, hearing. We use our senses to observe and learn the process of communications.

Many of the people who study public speaking today take courses that are based on outdated approaches. Even contemporary "experts" still teach by the methods of thirty or forty years ago. Famous comedian and talk show host Steve Allen wrote a book on how to give a speech, but the best way to learn how to give a speech is to watch Steve on television. There he's at his best in conversation, and *good speech is good conversation whether you're seated or standing.*

Television techniques are exciting, loose, and comfortable. That's why when my associate, Jon Kraushar, and I teach communications, we don't use rigid rules or repetitive exercises. We avoid drills. We don't use textbooks. But we *do* use video. Because if you can see yourself doing something well and can re-create it the next time you get up, you'll improve over and over again. Compared to the textbook method, it's like the difference between reading about how to swing a golf club and watching a video of yourself swinging a golf club. There's no substitute for the hands-on approach. You try, you watch yourself, then you refine.

ORGANIC SPEECH

As a consultant to a major broadcasting company, I traveled to various cities to evaluate television talk show hosts. I spent time with each of them and watched them on the air at their stations. But even before meeting them for the first time, I'd check into a hotel and watch their programs on television, with the sound turned off, for five or ten minutes. If there was nothing happening on the screen in the way the host looked or moved that made me interested enough to stand up and turn the sound up, then I knew that the host was not a great television performer. I'd watch the screen for interesting expressions on people's faces, sudden movement, laughter, or whatever made me say to myself, "Hey, I wonder what's going on here? I want to reach over and turn the sound up." If nothing moved me toward that sound knob, I would often recommend terminating the contract of that performer.

There may be some ex–television hosts somewhere in America who are gagging while reading this because they now know that they lost their jobs because some guy was sitting in a hotel room watching the television set with the sound off. However, this is a technique that I still use today with clients in our training course.

If you have access to videotape, ask someone to interview you. Then turn the sound down and watch yourself. Are you still interesting? Or place a mirror by your telephone. Watch yourself as you speak *and* listen. Do your eyes and face look engaged and lively? Do you gesture when you speak? Do you ever smile?

People who are the best communicators communicate with their whole being. They're animated, expressive, interesting to watch—just as they *should* be on television. Once you recognize these changes in communications techniques brought about by television, you can take some of the basics of video-age communications and transfer them to a meeting in your office, a business negotiation, or a sale to a client. Certainly, you should speak loudly enough for your listeners to hear, and of course you should look at them. You should gesture. But none of these things will work for you unless they're organic, meaning that they come from within. Employing communications techniques in a mechanical fashion only makes you seem wooden, and you'll be seen as insincere.

You can't force a smile. Many people think that smiling is just a matter of moving the facial muscles. But it's much more than that. It's triggered by emotions generated from thought. Stop for a moment and think of someone who makes you smile. Think of an incident in your life that was funny. Think of a time when you truly laughed. As you close your eyes and recall these experiences, your face will change. It will soften. The smile comes naturally. When a photographer says, "Smile," people often produce forced grins. If you just concentrate on someone you like, who makes you happy, your face will automatically smile. And it will be real. Remember: Smiling is first in the brain, *then* on the face.

VOCAL VARIETY: THE SPICE OF SPEECH

Our voices are much more flexible than we think. We often have a much wider vocal range than we realize. I'm reminded of an actor I once worked with who turned out to be one of the best impressionists in the world—Frank Gorshin. I was told that when he was young and first starting out in the business, he went to a nightclub with a friend to see a hypnotist. The hypnotist selected Gorshin from the audience to come up on stage, hypnotized him, and then told him that he was Kirk Douglas and other movie stars such as Burt Lancaster and Clark Gable. Although Gorshin hadn't yet made a career as an impressionist, amazingly, in front of the audience, he imitated those actors with an almost exact replication of their voices, rhythms, and styles.

That night, Frank Gorshin the impressionist was born. When the hypnotist brought him out of the trance, Gorshin found that he could mimic those and other famous voices. He had a terrific ear and wonderful control of his voice. He built a spectacular career as an impressionist, entertaining audiences worldwide.

Gorshin expanded his talents into an acting career, but he really got launched because a hypnotist cleared his mind of what he thought he couldn't do and allowed him to use his voice in a new way. It had always been physically possible, but he had never known it. All of us have a much broader vocal range than we realize. We must clear our minds and avoid concentrating on what we can't do. We should be open to what we *can* do.

WORDS AND MUSIC

Mark Twain was a renowned speaker in his day as well as a famous writer. One morning as he was dressing, he found a button missing from his shirt. Annoyed, he took another shirt. But it was also short a button. Exasperated, he took a third shirt from his bureau. It, too, lacked a button.

Twain flew into a rage, swearing like a stevedore. When he was through, he was startled to see his wife standing at the door, fuming in her own way at his intemperance. Carefully, slowly, and without a trace of emotion, she repeated every obscene word just uttered by her husband.

That took several minutes. When she was through, she stood impassive and silent, hoping her display would shame Twain. Instead, with a twinkle in his eye, he puffed on his cigar and said, "My dear, you have the words, but you don't have the music."

The voice, like the smile, is shaped by a combination of muscles and emotions. My experience is that you can improve your voice more by working on emotional expression than on mechanical drills. Let's say, though, that you commit months or years of your life to visiting a speech therapist twice a week, and you work on the often recommended, boring, and repetitive vocal drills. You can, in fact, expand and improve your voice.

The drills *will* work, if *you* work that hard. But in twenty-six years of working in this field, I've never met anyone who actually practiced those drills, except one man who locked himself in a room and tried to do the la-la-la drills every night. His wife divorced him.

TAPE AND APE

But don't despair. There *are* some practical, nonrepetitive things you can do to improve your voice. One alternative to the conventional drills is to tape-record random excerpts of yourself speaking on the phone. Then play the tape back. Listen for common vocal problems such as nasality, unnaturally high or low pitch, mumbling, breathiness, or sibilance. To overcome these problems, buy a tape of a famous actor or actress reading selections from literary works or speeches. Record yourself reading those same selections and compare your vocal quality. Your goal isn't to become a performer, but when you hear good speech and attempt to emulate it, you *will* improve your voice.

People who want to be radio announcers train their voices by taping the best professionals and trying, at first, to imitate the pros. The process is called "tape and ape." The goal isn't to become a mimic. It's to develop a *range* for the voice. Range, or vocal variety, should be your goal, too: It's what makes a voice interesting, alive, and distinctive. Just as you'd watch a tape of Jack Nicklaus swinging a golf club to help perfect your own swing, or of Martina Navratilova swinging a tennis racquet to improve your backhand, you can do the same with recordings by professionals. You don't have to turn this into a second career. Fifteen minutes of practice a day will make dramatic improvements not only in your voice but in your pronunciation, articulation, and inflection.

IF YOU CARE, THEY CARE

As an alternative exercise, try this, using a video recorder or even an audio recorder. Tape yourself as you talk extemporaneously on a topic you really care about. Here's one possible topic: Recall the best vacation you ever had in your life. Assume you're talking to people looking for a great getaway. Your job is to convince them that they should go where you went, see what you saw, feel what you felt, understand why you liked it so much. Do that for five minutes and tape it. Replaying the tape, you'll hear your voice move up and down the musical scale. There will be lots of vocal variety because you relish the topic.

Here are some variations of this exercise. If you're a business executive, describe to your friends the best business deal you ever made: how it happened, why it happened, what you did that was right, and how you felt about it. Or describe the person who had the most influence on your life. Explain why. Your audience: a group of teenagers, either from an honor society or from a street gang. If you're able to paint a verbal picture with some emotion, you'll hear your voice move automatically. Keep this in mind every time you have to give a speech. If *you* care, your listeners will care and your voice will automatically move up and down gracefully and naturally. If you *don't* care, it will automatically flatten out and be b-o-r-i-n-g. And whether you're talking on the phone, running a meeting, or giving a speech, the last thing you want is a dull, monotonous voice that puts people to sleep.

ABSORB/PROJECT

William Jennings Bryan, a nineteenth-century American states-man, was famous for filling halls with his stentorian tones. He once spoke to a large audience for over three hours. Can you imagine that today? The old-fashioned William Jennings Bryan "school of oratory" taught that you must project yourself—in other words, "throw" your voice and gesture theatrically. I say that you must *absorb* what's going on *before* you can project. It's much like a programmer at a TV network. He decides who his audience is before he puts together a television show.

When you enter a communications situation, don't immediately stand up and start projecting your voice and throwing out your opinions. Stop for a second. Absorb what's going on. What's the mood of the room, the crowd—are they down, up, happy, expectant? Read what people are feeding back to you. Are they skeptical or eager?

Look at their eyes. Listen to them. Watch their breathing. Are they relaxed? Excited? Notice how they sit. What does their body language tell you? Do they move their chairs away from you or toward you? Do they lean forward or back? Are they anxious to learn from you or do they radiate a "show me" attitude?

Should you start with small talk and relax them before you get to the meat of the message? Or do you need to come in, grab them by the throat, and throw them to the floor with an arresting fact, statement, or story?

LAUNCHING

There are many ways to open a speech, including the use of humor, anecdotes, startling and relevant facts, apt quotations, historical references, rhetorical questions, and audience participation.

Here's an example of a speech opening that combines a number of these elements. It's adapted from a talk by Gerald C. Myers, chairman of the American Motors Corporation, before the Society of American Business and Economic Writers:

> I'll start with a medieval morality tale—a story about how important it is to have a sense of direction.
>
> The story is about a knight who returned to the castle at twilight in a state of total disarray. Dented armor, helmet falling off, face bloody, horse crippled, and the knight himself about to fall off the limping horse.
>
> "What hath befallen you, Sir Knight?" asked the lord of the castle.
>
> "Oh, sire," answered the knight, "I have been labouring in your service, robbing and plundering and pillaging your enemies in the West."

"You've what?" cried the lord. "I don't have any enemies in the West."

"Oh," said the knight. "You do now!"

There's a strong parallel in the recent history of the American car market. It lost its sense of direction, too.[3]

Whether you use humor, historical references, or any other attention-getting opening device, you should be comfortable with the style and content. It should fit *your* style.

You might like the simple, direct approach, used by John R. Beckett of Transamerica Corporation: "This morning I will be talking about five subjects: customers, employees, education, executives, and the importance of the 'concept of commitment.' "[4] Or you might prefer a "breezy" approach, as taken by banker David Rockefeller before the Los Angeles World Affairs Council: "Coming to Southern California is a delightful way to begin the spring, although your kind invitation might have been even more welcome in the dead of winter. At that time, however, I understand this area was being hit by floods, mud slides and earth tremors. Somebody probably figured that the last thing you needed was a great gust of wind from the East."[5]

Robert O. Skovgard, editor of *The Executive Speaker* newsletter, offers this helpful list of tips for opening a speech:

- Use comparisons, examples, illustrations, and anecdotes.
- Use familiar, concrete language; avoid general and abstract wording.
- Use "fireplug" words (short, bright, utilitarian).
- Use picturesque, image-producing words.
- Rely on simple subject-verb order.
- Stay with one idea per sentence.
- Use no more than one dependent clause per sentence.
- Make frequent use of transition words.
- Use conversational language (first-person pronouns, contractions, short words, sentence fragments, simple sentences, questions, action verbs, personal anecdotes).[6]

Incidentally, every one of these suggestions for making you more effective in a formal speaking situation also will work in informal communications situations—whether you're chatting with friends over dinner, mingling with new acquaintances at a cocktail party, or participating in a business meeting.

THE EYES

The conventional advice to establish eye contact with your audience is fine. But that does not mean combing the crowd with your eyes like a minesweeper. It means using your eyes to absorb, to detect nuances, and to help you adjust your communications accordingly. If you're afraid to look at the members of the audience (for example, if you never look up from reading a text), they won't be very impressed with you regardless of your words. If you stare blankly at them or at a point at the back of the room, they won't feel you've reached them.

What you should do is break the audience down and treat it as a collection of individuals. Look at individual people as you speak. In the beginning of the speech, look at one person who has a friendly, warm face, because that will help put you at ease. But as the speech progresses, look at small groups of people all through the audience and continue to talk. Do this purposefully. As you move from small group to small group— or from individual to individual—in the audience, linger for a few seconds and talk just to that person or just to that small group of people as if you were having a "miniconversation" with them. This should not be done in any kind of a predictable pattern, but in a random fashion, so that it doesn't look staged.

Again, common sense prevails. The eyes should be used when speaking to a large group the same way they would be used when speaking to a small group. When you're sitting in a room with four or five other people, from time to time you glance at one or the other person and carry on part of the conversation with that person. It's exactly the same when you're on your feet in front of a large crowd.

SAY WHAT THE AUDIENCE THINKS

Every speech situation is different. Often I stand up in front of a crowd with a prepared opening, and as soon as I get to the lectern I realize—because something feels strange—that the prepared opening simply won't work, and that if I stick with my text, it's going to bomb. I have to deal with what happened before I came on and how the audience is feeling now.

I've seen speakers get up at the end of a long evening, after the emcee has read the treasurer's report and has introduced everybody in the room. By then, the members of the audience are thinking about their baby-sitters and whether the hubcaps have been stolen off their cars in the parking lot. What you really need to do at that point is lighten it up, let them know that you're aware of how they feel. Tell them that you recognize the hour is late and you're not going to keep them too long. You want to move immediately into the text and relax them. If the time is short, don't talk *faster*. Talk *less*. Edit your text.

A couple of years ago, I was the last speaker at a particularly long dinner where more than fifty people had received awards. The entire audience was thinking the same thing: "When will this be over? How many more of these can there be?" I got up and said, "Before I actually start my speech, I'd like each of you who got awards to stand up again one at a time so that we can recognize you."

Of course, the place broke up in laughter because everyone in the audience felt that the evening had gone on too long. By kidding about the situation, I became one of them and they became more receptive to the rest of my speech. It's a matter of sensing or feeling what's going on, and perceiving how best to get to the audience. Absorb first, then project.

FEELINGS

In every communications situation—one-on-one or in a group—you should be asking yourself, "What am I feeling here?" Whenever I'm confused in a business situation, I generally get very quiet, sit back, and ask myself, "How do I feel about what's going on here?" If I'm in a conversation with one person, I might ask myself, "How do I feel about this person?" The emphasis is first on my feelings.

On occasion I'll sit in a meeting where some poor guy makes his presentation and the boss is totally turned off. If I sense that nothing good is going to happen that day, I don't present my ideas. I just get off the playing field, because my intuition tells me there is no chance for progress. You may only get one chance to present your idea, so don't waste it if the recipient is not tuned in to you.

Once, during a strategy meeting for a U.S. Senate race, we listened to a presentation by the campaign's television-time buyer. The campaign manager was a woman I'll call Betty, who was in her early seventies, a very sharp lady, very tough.

The various consultants to this campaign were at war over certain strategies and procedures. At one point, I just happened to see Betty flinch—just the slightest movement of the head sideways and narrowing of the eyes. She felt somebody was wrong in something they were saying. It might have been me, it might have been someone else, but something was wrong. I stopped the meeting.

"Wait a minute. Betty, what's going on in your mind? Because if you're uncomfortable with something, we need to know about it."

She hadn't even been aware of her reaction. "Well, I don't like these budget numbers," she said. "We just won't be able to raise that much money!"

We solved the problem then and there. Believe me, it would have been major chaos later if that little twitch of her head hadn't tipped me off that there was a problem.

BETWEEN THE LINES

I was recently visiting at a friend's home, and his wife came into the room. I said, "How are you?"

As she answered gaily, "I'm fine," her eyes shifted away from me. She continued, "Everything's great. How are you?" But her voice was falsely gay, very forced and high-pitched, very tight. I knew there was some problem.

The nature of the problem isn't important, but this situation illustrates my point. While her words said everything was all right, everything else about her said she was under a tremendous amount of stress. I noticed throughout the evening that when she was talking naturally about an abstract subject, her pitch was comfortable and much lower. Whenever the subject turned to her personal life or her relationship with the family, however, her pitch went up dramatically, and her voice tightened. By her forced, determined effort to project that everything was okay, she instead revealed the information which she was so desperately trying to hide—that things *weren't* all that great.

You've probably been in a situation where you've read tension between two other people. Although they weren't even speaking directly to each other, much less arguing overtly, you sensed hostility. Or have you ever been sitting in a room with your back to the door and sensed when someone else entered, even though you didn't hear them?

BREAKING THROUGH

We all have the capability to read, or sense, what's happening with others. This ability is every bit as accurate and reliable as the sensory abilities of the eyes and ears, and it is often more important in forming your final assessment of what's going on. It can often give you the edge when negotiating with another person.

Here's an example. As a TV producer, I remember being called into a union negotiation to discuss a labor issue that could have resulted in throwing a lot of people out of work. I knew the situation was serious, but when things are tense, I have a tendency to use humor to relax myself and others. So I wasn't taking myself or the labor leaders very seriously. I made a few side remarks under my breath to test the atmosphere. They were harmless and meant as jokes. Most of the union negotiators stared straight ahead. But I noticed that one man thought what I had said was pretty funny and he was chuckling. I knew he was powerful and realized he might be an ally. I looked at him and there was instantly some rapport between us.

The next time we took a break from the negotiation, I caught up with him at the coffee machine and asked him to take a walk with me outside. I said to him, "Look, we've got a lot of 'experts' in there who could mess this thing up and hurt a lot of people. I think you and I can work this out so that we don't set any harmful precedents for the union. Just give me what I need to get the show done and we'll keep everybody working."

We worked things out right there in the alley behind the television studio. We went back into the meeting and within an hour we had an agreement to continue working. The only reason that happened was because I was watching him closely and realized he was basically a good guy who wanted to get this problem solved, and he had a sense of humor. We were reading each other, absorbing each other's signals, and developing a rapport which allowed us to solve the problem.

THE NONSTOP TALKER

Some people have never developed the ability to read others. These people are generally too focused on themselves. For example, a client who wanted to run for Congress came in to see my associate, Jon Kraushar. Jon asked me to join them, and what followed was amazing. The prospective client talked nonstop about himself for two hours!

He was so boring that I left the room three different times. Each time I came back, he was still talking. He was so unwilling to listen and so unaware of what was going on around him that I could have gone out to lunch and he would have just kept on going. As Voltaire wrote, "The secret of being a bore is to tell everything." We've all met people like this man—maybe not as extreme, but nonetheless insensitive to others.

Gradually he learned how to strike enough of a balance between talking and listening to get elected. Good communicators adjust their talk-listen ratio to the situation. A good rule of thumb is to listen 60 percent and talk 40 percent of the time. As psychologist Carl Rogers wrote, "Man's inability to communicate is a result of his failure to listen effectively, skillfully, and with understanding to another person." And as Wilson Mizner said, "A good listener is not only popular everywhere, but after a while he knows something."

YOUR LISTENING RATIO

Do you talk more than you listen? Rate yourself on the talk-listen ratio chart. Then ask two family members and two friends to score you. Also, have your boss or two coworkers score you.

Check the line of the ratio best representing the percentage of the time you generally:

Talk	Listen	
10	90	_____
20	80	_____
30	70	_____
40	60	_____
50	50	_____
60	40	_____
70	30	_____
80	20	_____
90	10	_____

Compare your self-assessment with the way others rated you. If there are major discrepancies in the scores, the more accurate numbers are the ones reflecting how others view you. Their perception is what's real.

In general, though, you should strive to listen 60 to 70 percent of the time and talk 30 to 40 percent. The reason for this bias toward listening is that most people listen but don't really *hear*. We therefore need to overcompensate—and listen more—to improve our comprehension. We'll explain this in more detail in the next chapter.

5

POOR RECEPTION

How good are you at listening? Much has been written on the subject, but a few simple techniques will help you learn this skill. It will enrich your life as well as those around you. According to listening experts like Dr. Lyman K. Steil of the University of Minnesota, Americans spend 9 percent of the time they devote to communication each day in writing, 16 percent in reading, 30 percent in speaking, and 45 percent in listening.

However, most people are inefficient listeners. Tests indicate that right after listening to a ten-minute oral presentation, the average listener has heard, comprehended, accurately evaluated, and retained about half of what was said. Within forty-eight hours, that drops another 50 percent to a 25 percent effectiveness level. By the end of a week, that level goes down to about 10 percent or less.

A TALLY OF LOSSES

Up to 80 percent of a spoken message gets lost or garbled by the time it travels from the executive level to the sales level of a company. To quote Dr. Steil's findings as reported by the Sperry Corporation, "With more than 100 million workers in America, a simple 10-dollar listening mistake by each of them would cost a billion dollars. Letters have to be retyped, appointments rescheduled, shipments reshipped."

At one of New England Telephone's twelve divisions, it was

found that around 20 percent of its operator-assisted calls were delayed by listening problems. The average delay was just fifteen seconds. But that cost the division $874,800 a year. New England Telephone estimated that it recovered about $500,000 of that loss after it developed a program to teach effective listening.

According to a news story headlined IF ONLY CON ED LISTENED, the electrical blackout of New York City in July of 1977 could have been prevented if Consolidated Edison had only heeded a warning from the State Power Pool. In a taped conversation, a Power Pool spokesperson told a Con Ed worker, "You'd better get rid of some [electrical] load." The worker reportedly replied, "You're right, you're right!" But somebody didn't listen. Some thirty-two minutes later, New York City went pitch-black.

We're not trained to listen. As children, basically we hear threats. When Mother says, "Okay. I've said it for the third time. Now this time you're going to get a spanking," or "This time you're going to bed," we say, "Oh, sure." From our earliest days, people have had to figuratively hit us over the head with a sledgehammer to get our attention, and parents oftentimes play right into our hands. They start yelling when they want something, instead of quietly saying, "I'm going to ask you to do this, and I'm only going to ask you once. And this is what I would like done. Listen very carefully. Now what did I say to you?" Either the child can repeat it or he can't, but he immediately knows he has to listen carefully. That doesn't mean being cruel. You don't have to do it in a militaristic manner. But if you teach your children to listen, they'll be more successful in life.

TRY LISTENING

Let's assume that you've been told or have decided that you're a poor listener, and you want to get better at it. What are some of the things you could do?

Try going to a week of meetings and saying absolutely nothing unless you're directly asked to speak or you're required to talk. Do nothing else but concentrate and focus on what other people say. Listen to what they say and what you think they really mean. Take notes to determine whether what they said and what they meant struck you as being different, since oftentimes people say one thing but mean something else.

For a week, discipline yourself to go with a notepad to any meeting or interactive situation and listen. Toward the end of the week, occasionally ask questions to elicit more information. Then try to figure out what you've learned during that period of time.

Watch to see if the face, eyes, voice, and body reinforce the speaker's words or detract from them. Look for telltale, non-verbal signs that suggest a conflict between what's said and what's meant. Although there's no hard-and-fast cause-effect relationship between body language and intent, often people who are suspicious glance sideways. Those who are nervous may fidget or clear their throat. If someone peers over his glasses he may be evaluating you. Conversely, if someone leans forward, smiles at you, and unbuttons his jacket, he is probably receptive and willing to cooperate with you.

You have to just sit quietly for a while, listen, and see what other people are saying. According to the ancient text Sirach, "If you love to listen, you will gain knowledge and if you incline your ear, you will become wise."

BE SPECIFIC

Are others listening to you? How can you be sure that when you've given someone instructions, they've actually heard you, and your instructions will be followed?

That's a common problem, especially in business, because most people are not very good at giving instructions or orders—they don't set time lines, they're not specific. Let's say there's a problem with a client. The boss may tell a subordinate, "Take care of that and get back to me." Now the boss thinks she's said, "Call the client. Gather all of the pertinent information. Identify the problem. Solve it if you can. If you can't, come back to me and tell me what the problem is and I'll solve it. And do it today."

What the employee heard was "There may be a problem with that client. I guess I should give them a call in the next few days, and then get back to the boss. Well . . . maybe I'll just wait till she brings it up again."

Imagine there is a Dictaphone on the desk when that conversation takes place. The boss pushes the record button before the meeting starts. In doing so, she says to the subordinate, "I want to tape this because I'm trying to improve my communication skills. I'm trying to be very specific about what our problem is with the client. What do you think it is?"

The boss then listens to the subordinate describe the problem. Let's say it's an inaccurate description, but it's the subordinate's best description. The boss then tries to focus on what the client's problem is. She poses certain questions like "Have you talked to the client? When did you talk to the client? What specifically did the client say? Do you recall his words? How urgent do you think this situation is? What would you recommend as a way of solving it? Do you feel that I need to get into it at this point, or can you solve it?" Then, "I think it's important. What I would like you to do is call the client today and get the parameters of the problem. Tell the client, 'The last time that I talked with you I got the feeling there was a problem. I'd like you to outline what the problem is, because we'd sure like to solve it for you.' Let the client talk. Ask questions so he'll be specific. And say, 'All right. We can solve those things one-two-three. We'll get back to you.' "

To put a time line on the subordinate's mission (to monitor how well he listened), the boss could then tell the subordinate, "This is now Thursday. By Monday I'd like to have a report from you on how this was handled."

LISTENING TIPS

The British author Rudyard Kipling had this to say about asking the right questions to get the right answers: "I keep six honest serving men./(They taught me all I knew);/Their names are What and Why and When/And How and Where and Who." Make sure you've carefully considered all six of Kipling's "honest" factors when you listen. It will serve you well.

Here are some tips to help you become a better listener:

1. Relax and clear your mind if someone is speaking, so that you're receptive to what they're saying.

2. Never assume that you've heard correctly because the first few words have taken you in a certain direction. Most listening mistakes are made by people who only hear the first few words of a sentence, finish the sentence in their own minds, and miss the second half.

3. Learn to speed up your point of contact as a listener. The second you hear a sound coming from another person, concentrate quickly on the first few words. That will get you started correctly.

4. Don't tune out a speaker just because you don't like his or her looks, voice, or general demeanor. Stay open to new information.

5. Don't overreact emotionally to the speaker's words or ideas—especially those that may run contrary to your usual thinking. Hear the other person out.

6. Before forming a conclusion, let the speaker complete his or her thought. Then evaluate by distinguishing in your mind specific evidence presented (good) versus generalities (bad).

7. Part of listening is writing things down that are important. You should always have a piece of paper, a pencil, a notebook, or a card in your pocket. Throughout the day, many important things are discussed. But by the close of business, you don't remember the details. How many of you have found a phone number on a scrap of paper in your handwriting with no name attached? So take notes to listen, to remember later, and to document, if necessary.

8. People will often say one thing and mean something else. As you grow in your listening sophistication, it is important

to listen for *intent* as well as *content*. This gets back to the absorption process we talked about before. Watch as you listen. Be sure that the speaker's eyes, body, and face are sending signals that are consistent with the speaker's voice and words. If something sounds out of sync, get it cleared up. Many people are afraid of looking foolish if they ask for clarification because it will seem as if they weren't paying attention. Better to have the speaker repeat a message on the spot than to set off a chain reaction of misunderstanding.

9. Human communication goes through three phases: reception (listening), information processing (analyzing), and transmission (speaking). When you overlap any of those, you may short-circuit the reception (listening) process. Try to listen without *over*analyzing. Try to listen without interrupting the speaker.

10. Another major failing of people in listening is simple distraction. To listen correctly you must be able to reprioritize immediately. The second you hear sound coming toward you, focus and say to yourself, "This is important." Keep your eye on the speaker. Don't fiddle with pens, pencils, papers, or other distractions.

If you're able to follow these ten steps, you will eventually be an excellent listener.

THE WORDS GET IN THE WAY

The flip side of listening too little is talking too much. The world is full of people who tell you how to build a clock when all you asked for was the time of day. One executive I know was very much this way. He was bright and well educated. When he came to me, he was being groomed by the president of the company to be his successor, because the president liked him very much.

The man's problem was that he couldn't close a sale. After working with him, I discovered that it was virtually impossible for him to cut to the heart of anything. He rarely got to the bottom line. He would always talk around the point and tell you a lot more than you needed to know. Eventually, he would just wear you out.

He blew sales because he didn't absorb. He didn't listen. He didn't observe. He missed the signals that the prospect was ready to buy. He would just keep talking. I had to teach him to do more listening than talking, but first I had to convince him that he had a problem. The only way I could do this was to videotape him in a conversation answering questions that I asked him.

In one case I asked him a question and his answer went on for over five minutes. He not only answered the question I asked him but answered three questions I didn't ask him, two of which were not to his advantage. Even after I showed him the video-tape, he rationalized and made excuses for all the talk. So I had a transcript made of the actual conversation. I made him sit and read the transcript out loud.

Once he did that, he became so embarrassed that he was convinced he had a problem. I then asked him to rewrite the answer to the question in the briefest form possible. It turned out that he came up with an excellent answer in three sentences which took exactly nineteen seconds.

TALK LESS

A general rule of thumb: Most of us talk more than we need to. Most of us tell people more than they need to know. Most of us ramble too much, and most of us take too long to say things. If you accept this, you can begin to clean up your conversation and become someone people want to listen to, instead of someone they feel they have to listen to. The moral: If most of the time you talk more than you listen, you're probably failing in your communication, and you're probably boring people, too.

6

THE FOUR ESSENTIALS
OF A GREAT
COMMUNICATOR

There are only four things people you communicate with won't forgive you for: not being prepared, comfortable, committed, and interesting. Remember the first time you stood up in class to make a presentation? You might have been in the fifth grade. Your teacher, who was very strict, called your name, and your heart sank. Let's go back in time and eavesdrop. I don't mean to poke fun. After all, there but for the grace of God go all of us.

However, there's fat Henry, with his runny nose and one sneaker untied. When it was his turn, he blushed so red that his face blended in with his freckles. There's Rhonda, who stood frozen to the spot, afraid to smile because her braces made her mouth look like a barbed-wire fence. Then there's Mort, the class "brain," who wore his bow tie for the occasion but spoke with his eyes fluttering like a hummingbird's wings.

In fifth grade, moments like these can traumatize you. Hopefully, we can all laugh now. But for many of us, it's still a nervous laugh.

Many people had a mortifying experience the first time they

gave a formal speech—and they've never gotten over it. In a later chapter, we're going to examine the problems of stage fright and other anxieties associated with public speaking. But right now, I want to tell you about four things that audiences (no matter how large) won't forgive in a speaker. If you concentrate on getting these few things right, most, if not all, of your fears about addressing audiences will disappear. And you'll become an accomplished communicator. Remember, the essentials don't change because the situation changes. These things work in interpersonal communications as well as in formal speeches.

These four elements—"the four essentials"—are simple. But they're not necessarily easy. However, if you keep them in mind in every communication situation and practice them, you'll automatically get better.

THE FIRST ESSENTIAL: BE PREPARED

Preparation is essential because whenever you speak to other people they must have absolute confidence that you know what you're talking about. That doesn't mean you have to be the world's leading authority on the subject. But your listeners should feel that you know more about the subject than they do and that you've done some preparation for addressing them—either formally or informally.

A U.S. senator had a man on his staff who was an excellent speechwriter. One day the speechwriter, a rather shy young man, said to the senator, "Sir, I think things have been going quite well. The speeches I've written for you have been widely praised for their style and content. So I'd like a raise." The senator replied in a huff, "Just keep writing the speeches." And he refused him the raise.

The next day, the senator had a major address on television, and he started reading the first page of the speech. "Today," he intoned, "I'm going to tell you about the four major problems we face as a nation," and he went down his list. Then he said,

"Now I'm going to tell you what I propose as solutions to these problems." He turned the page, and it said, "Okay, you SOB, you're on your own!"

WHERE TO START

The first thing an audience (no matter how small or large) won't forgive you for is acting like that senator—failing to be prepared. I learned about preparation from my good friend Pearl Bailey. No performer in the world made it look so easy. Pearlie Mae, as she was known, even put on bedroom slippers in the middle of her act and sat in a rocking chair. She'd tell you how tired she was, wander around the stage, and talk to the band and the audience.

A casual observer would think she was absolutely winging it as she went along. But I've been at a Pearl Bailey rehearsal. The woman was a consummate professional. She mastered every note of music the band played. She knew the timing of every drumbeat. She measured the stage with her eyes so she knew exactly how far she could move. She knew where the lights hit, where her positioning tape marks were on the floor. She was aware of the sight lines of the audience and she controlled the rhythm of the whole act.

In rehearsal, she was as cool and tough as a Marine Corps drill sergeant. She was always pleasant, but she was also tough. She was so meticulous in rehearsal that she could afford to make it look easy once the show started. And when she performed, she was great.

I often think about her as I coach people to perform. Most people try to avoid the most important part—a little rehearsal. If they would just spend 20 percent of the time Pearl Bailey did getting ready, they'd be a lot better at "show time." Not only must you be prepared, but you should do at least some of the preparation yourself, even if you're a busy top-level executive.

Whether you work alone to prepare for a meeting or to give

a speech or whether you have some outside help, you should begin by assessing the knowledge, interests, and needs of your listeners. Ask yourself: Why have I been asked to speak? What is expected of me on this occasion? How can I apply my special experience to the concerns of my listeners? Dictate or write your thoughts first without editing them. Then go back and polish the material.

SPEAK THE SPEECH

Another very important point of preparation is going over the speech out loud before you give it, so that you can change any words or phrases that you stumble over. If you do this, you're almost guaranteed to do well.

Haven't we all heard speakers who were unprepared? We feel embarrassed for the speaker and angry and frustrated that our time has been wasted.

NO COP-OUTS

Interestingly enough, many people who would not accept excuses from subordinates or coworkers about a poorly thought out and sloppily prepared assignment will cop out themselves in the most amateurish way about giving a speech or preparing a presentation for a business meeting. "Well, I didn't have time. No, I didn't rehearse it out loud. No, I didn't look at it until I was on my way to the event. The speechwriter didn't write what I wanted." Well, these excuses are unacceptable. Why didn't the person delivering the remarks correct these things?

If you find yourself making excuses, ask yourself these questions: What am I afraid of? Do I have performance anxiety? Am I afraid of being judged? Is this speech or appearance important enough to demand some of my time or can I assign it to a subordinate? If I don't prepare and rehearse, what kind of example does that set for those who look up to me for inspiration or leadership?

A PREPARATION CHECKLIST

Please don't be intimidated by the length of the following checklist for preparing a speech from an outline—the ideal method. The checklist will save you time in preparing your next speech.

A. Preparing

1. *Evaluate your audience.* Be aware, in advance, of their special interests, expertise, and desires or aspirations, so you can be sure to address them appropriately.

2. *Consider the occasion.* Your approach can be influenced by an event celebrated by the group, such as a holiday, anniversary, retirement, or announcement.

3. *Determine the length of your talk.* Always come in a bit shorter than you're budgeted, and your audience will be surprised—and grateful.

4. *Determine the purpose* of your speech:
   a. To entertain
   b. To inform
   c. To inspire
   d. To persuade

Good speeches often combine elements of all four.

5. *Decide on a central theme* that can be written down in a single sentence. If you can't write your *theme* on the back of a business card, it's too complicated.

6. To aid your confidence, *develop background knowledge* in the speech area. You must do some of your own preparation.

7. *Gather facts.* Do research. Be sure your remarks are relevant to the interests of the group.

8. *Consider the makeup of the audience* and its present attitude toward you. For hostile or skeptical audiences, you will need to show that you understand all sides of the issue. For supportive audiences, your job is to reaffirm values.

9. *Find a good opening line* or story that relates to the speech. If it doesn't interest you, it won't interest your audience.

10. *Possible speech structures* include:

Past—Present—Future

Write down three to five questions the audience might ask of you—and answer them as the body of your speech

B. A Sample Speech Outline

INTRODUCTION	I. Anecdote, shocking statement, or the like
(Tell them what you're going to tell them)	A. Transition line (relate the opening to the audience and tell why you are speaking)
BODY	II. Expansion of theme established by opening
(Tell them)	A. Supportive facts
	B. Supportive facts
	1. Subpoints of A and B
	2. Same
	3. Same
	C. Transition to close
CLOSE	III. Summary
(Tell them what you've told them—and close the "sale")	A. Final point you want to leave audience with (call to action)

Make your speech outline simple: triple-spaced and easy to read.

C. Speech Delivery
1. After the outline is made, develop wording of certain thoughts, including some memorable phrases and quotes. Be interesting!

2. Support statements with facts, examples, analogies, and so forth.

3. Practice the speech out loud into a tape recorder (vital to success).

4. Time the speech. Guesstimate 20 percent longer for actual delivery time to allow for the unexpected.

5. Consider the size of the audience you'll be speaking to and practice to reach the back row (enough volume, but don't shout or strain).

6. Take your time to get the audience's attention before beginning your speech. Pause, then look up to establish eye contact.

7. Listen to your speech on audio or video recorder for voice transitions:
  a. Rate or tempo changes
  b. Sincerity
  c. Intensity
  d. Volume
  e. Inflection (highs and lows)
  f. Pronunciation
  g. Drama (silences, shifts in pace)
  h. Whether you sound confident

8. Rehearse it again out loud and be sure you have good eye contact. Can you lift your head from the outline without losing your place?

9. The more you rehearse out loud, the better the speech will be.

MAKE IT YOUR OWN

It's important to make the material your own. President Reagan was a master at that. He'd go through his speechwriter's material word by word, inserting his own ideas and phrasing. That may not even require a lot of time. Some of my clients can do it in half an hour at most, if they have a rough draft of their remarks. But many senior executives are just afraid they can't do it, so they stay away from it completely. Whether you're facing the board of directors or the PTA, your professional reputation is on the line—you *must* get involved. This is a very important use of your time. Making a good impression for yourself and the organization you represent *is* part of your job description. Again, essential number one is *be prepared.*

THE SECOND ESSENTIAL:
MAKE OTHERS COMFORTABLE

To make others comfortable, you have to appear comfortable yourself. The best example of speaker comfort I've ever seen was a guest we had on "The Mike Douglas Show." He was, of all things, the complaint manager at a local department store in Cleveland. We were doing a Christmas show, and we thought it would be interesting to have a complaint manager tell about some of the unusual gifts people returned, why they brought them back, and what the complaints were. This particular man was a jovial fellow, totally comfortable with himself, even though he weighed in at about three hundred pounds.

We had an area in the studio where the host and guests sat, and on it there was a small raised platform called a gazebo with four or five chairs. We were doing television live in those days, and inventing the form as we went along.

This huge complaint manager walked in and sat down on one of those chairs on the platform. There were three or four other guests already seated. During the program, he rocked back and forth on the back legs of the chair. I noticed that one of the chair legs kept inching closer and closer to the edge of the platform. We were three or four minutes away from a commercial break. I just prayed that we'd get to the break before the chair got to the edge. I tried to write a cue card to warn Mike what was happening, but I couldn't get it across to him.

Finally, the inevitable happened. The leg went off the back edge of the platform, the chair tipped over backward, and right in midsentence this three-hundred-pound man rolled over, did a backward somersault, and disappeared out of sight. One instant he and Mike were talking, the next instant he was gone and there was a big hole in this group of people. The studio audience gasped.

Well, this guy was so comfortable with himself that he just picked himself up, picked up the chair, walked around in front, put down the chair, sat down, and without ever missing a beat continued the story he was telling. The audience and the whole television crew gave him a spontaneous standing ovation for coolness under fire. He was so comfortable throughout the whole episode that the audience just loved him. After that, he became somewhat of a regular on the show based on his ability to handle adversity with great comfort and aplomb.

WE'RE ONLY HUMAN

Most people would be so embarrassed by falling off the stage during a television program that they would never go on television again. I learned a lesson from that complaint manager twenty-two years ago and it has always stuck in my mind. We are all human. Accidents can happen. We are not perfect. We may even make fools of ourselves. But if we can smile and keep on going, we can win the audience.

The most successful senior executives I've seen are powerful but still able to make other people feel comfortable. John H. Bryan, Jr., chairman of Sara Lee Corporation, for instance, is a man who is deceptively casual in his approach to things. It is clear he has a razor-sharp mind and is capable of making very tough decisions, but he comes across as being very laid-back and relaxed. He can really make others feel at ease. He has a wonderful smile. He looks at you when he speaks to you.

GETTING COMFORTABLE

It's easy to say, "Be comfortable," but we have to define it a little bit further. And I'll help you work toward that goal. People who are comfortable and who also put others at ease don't overreact to events by getting uptight and causing others to do the same. If somebody comes into your office and tells you that a truck has just backed into your car and totaled it, it's natural to be upset. It is not natural to rant in front of the person who simply delivered the bad news to you. We often do this to other people: We get upset with them rather than putting their role and our feelings into perspective.

At work, I've seen people who are told that a package has been lost in the mail. They get livid. It sets off a chain reaction in the office. It ruins not only that person's day, but everybody else's day. In the meantime, someone else with a cool head has contacted the messenger or mail service and has put a tracer on the package. Nine times out of ten, it's found. If not, there's not a darned thing you can do about it anyway.

There's no use ruining the creative atmosphere of the office for the rest of the day. Yet you'd be surprised how many people can't keep their emotions under control. This makes other people uncomfortable and reduces their ability to communicate effectively. Some people actually believe a wild display of temper makes them appear more important, when in fact it always reduces their stature in others' eyes.

On the day of a speech, I try to stay clear of bad news and negative people. If I can't, I simply try to put the problem in context—in fact, I try to laugh at it. If I'm upset when I begin to speak, I'm going to make the audience uncomfortable.

If you're striving to be more comfortable yourself and to make others comfortable—especially in your interpersonal communications—one place to start is to accept others for who they are. You have two choices: You can act as though you tolerate people, or you can appreciate people. Those who appreciate people are going to make others more comfortable.

I've seen many situations in business in which someone comes to the boss with an idea. The idea won't work and may even be slightly crazy or counterproductive. Some bosses directly dress down the person—making the employee feel stupid. Other bosses just sit there with their arms crossed and a cold look in their eyes, communicating the message that the idea won't work.

Bosses who are the best communicators let the subordinate explain the idea. The boss first smiles and thanks the person for coming in with a suggestion. Then the boss uses a question-and-answer approach—a dialogue—to help the person think through the implications of the idea until it's apparent that it needs work. Getting positive reinforcement for the contribution, at least, makes the person comfortable—even motivated—to come up with a better idea. Isn't that the goal, anyway? If you make others uncomfortable, they may never approach you again. There's a cost to that—in morale and in the choking off of that one possible great idea in ten.

THE LIGHT TOUCH

A constructive way to make other people comfortable is to lighten up yourself. Take your job seriously but don't take yourself so seriously. This applies one-on-one or when you're talking to a larger audience. We'll discuss this in more detail in a later chapter. But humor is a way to take the sting out of almost anything and is used entirely too infrequently in the world. John F. Kennedy and Ronald Reagan are two people recalled for having the most serious job in the world yet being able to lighten it up—for themselves and for others. Here are examples of both the Kennedy and Reagan wits, from various stages of their careers.

QUESTION: (from a small boy) Senator Kennedy, how did you become a war hero?

SENATOR KENNEDY: It was involuntary. They sank my boat.[7]

REPORTER: Mr. President, have you narrowed your search for a new Postmaster General? Are you seeking a man with a business background or a political background?

PRESIDENT KENNEDY: The search is narrowing, but there are other fields still to be considered, including even a postal background.[8]

PRESIDENT REAGAN: I've been getting some flack about ordering the production of the B-1. How did I know it was an airplane? I thought it was a vitamin for the troops.[9]

PRESIDENT REAGAN: (to a group of doctors) We've made so many advances in my lifetime. For example, I have lived ten years longer than my life expectancy when I was born—a source of great annoyance to many people.[10]

OTHER POSITIVE ATTRIBUTES

Examples of the Kennedy and Reagan light touch have filled books. But even if you don't have a good sense of humor, you can still make others comfortable in other ways. You can become known as a person who is trustworthy. You can choose not to engage in gossip or sarcastic remarks about others when they are not present. You can avoid giving phony compliments but, whenever possible, say positive things about others.

You can practice looking more comfortable. Don't make sharp, jerky moves. At a lectern, don't rattle your papers. Avoid brushing back or fiddling with your hair, or pulling at your nose. These gestures convey a lack of comfort. Walk casually to the lectern, lay down your papers, place your hands on each side of the lectern, then look at the audience. Maintain your own timetable. If you overreact to the pressure of time, you will appear uncomfortable.

Ronald Reagan's greatest gift is not his speaking ability but his ability to make others comfortable. One day as we were getting started on his 1984 campaign, a half dozen of us were gathered in an informal meeting at the White House. Our jackets were off, ties askew, sleeves rolled up, coffee cups half empty, and ashtrays full.

Suddenly, without any announcement or fanfare, in strides the President of the United States. Commander in Chief of the Armed Forces. Leader of the Free World. Well, you never saw a bunch of grown men in repose shoot up faster and attempt to look dignified—with less dignity, I might add. Reagan just smiled, held up his hand as if to say, "Relax, guys," and breezily said, "Well, I figured as long as you were selling the soap, you might as well get a look at the bar." He chatted with us for a few minutes about the days when he was in advertising selling Borax and other products.

After fifteen minutes of conversation and banter he announced, with a twinkle in his eyes, "I guess I'd better get out of here before the mystique wears off." The president shook hands all around and walked out, as casually and self-assuredly as he had come in. The rest of our meeting took on a new sense of energy and purpose, because he had made everyone feel so comfortable.

A HARD CASE

Many of the executives who come to me have the problem of making other people uncomfortable without knowing that they're doing it, and it's my job to diagnose the causes and prescribe solutions. The most difficult client I've ever worked with was a fellow who simply could not see himself as others did. Everyone disliked him, and he rather liked himself. Actually, that's not quite true. Some people hated him. Consequently, my job was to explain to him in as diplomatic a manner as possible how people felt about him. This was difficult because I was starting to dislike him myself. I had to show him how and why this was happening, and then help him find some new ways of expressing himself.

His behavior was something like this. If you were talking about something he knew anything at all about, and he disagreed with you, he would curtly cut you off and jump down your throat with "You don't understand. I'll have to explain this to you." Or if you asked him a question that might have been covered in some printed material he'd given you, he would preface his response with "Well, obviously you didn't read the report I gave you. . . ." He continually lectured everyone. Even when he thought he was being polite he would begin with "Let me explain this to you." If he wasn't interested in what you were saying, he just looked bored and changed the subject. Do you know anyone like that? Have you ever acted like that yourself?

Suddenly it occurred to me to ask him if he'd ever been a teacher. "Yes," he said, "very early in my career I taught for a couple of semesters." And then it hit me that this was what was coming out. He was treating everyone as if they were students. The problem was that he was lecturing his peers and other members of the board of directors, who didn't appreciate being talked to in that manner. I tried to point out to him on videotape how he dealt with his peers and his superiors. Since he always took this lofty attitude, it wasn't easy to break through to him.

There was more to this man's problem than the fact that he had been a teacher. Most teachers don't treat their students in this manner. Psychologists would have a field day discussing his inferiority complex and his need to make himself feel bigger by making other people feel smaller. But my goal was to get him to operate effectively in the workplace. I did suggest that he might talk to a psychologist about why he needed to behave this way. In the meantime, I told him to stop it or, in my opinion, he would be fired. It's amazing how that statement can get some people's attention.

I finally said, "You're either going to have to start your own company, where you can be the supreme boss and behave any way you please, or you've got to alter your behavior."

Ultimately, after many videotape role-playing sessions he was able to change his behavior dramatically. He's sent me many clients since then, almost all from his senior management.

Once again, the second essential is to *make others comfortable*. Do you?

THE THIRD ESSENTIAL: BE COMMITTED

Being committed is crucial. Very few people freeze up, unable to speak, when they feel strongly about something. If you come home five nights in a row and your kid's bike is in the driveway, the first couple of times you mutter under your breath and move the bike. But the fifth time it happens, you say, "All right, that's it [vocal inflection]. Keep that bike [gesture] out of the driveway or I'm taking it away." You're very clear. Everything you may have learned about facial expression, eye contact, body language, and vocal energy come together, and everything clears up automatically with commitment.

That's why my course for executives avoids the traditional techniques. If you know what you are saying and why you are saying it, and you *care* about what you are saying, you will say it well! Another important point here is to know when you must do all of this. Know when you have to be good. Whether you're selling your ideas to the boss, meeting with your peers, or inspiring your troops, you should perform well. Obviously, it's not necessary 100 percent of the time, but whenever someone else's opinion of you counts, *you're on.* Be yourself—at your best.

Ordinary people become extraordinary communicators when they are fired up with commitment. This happened to Candy Lightner of Fair Oaks, California, after her thirteen-year-old daughter Cari was killed by a hit-and-run driver. The driver had been convicted of drunken driving and related offenses three times in four years—each time getting his license back after a slap on the wrist from the courts. Two days before he killed young Cari, the driver was arrested for another hit-and-run while intoxicated. He was released on bail.

Candy Lightner was told by a hard-bitten cop, "Lady, you'll be lucky if this guy gets any jail time—much less prison."

Grief-stricken, angry, and frustrated, Candy Lightner became committed to preventing others from being victimized like her daughter.

Although divorced and supporting two other young children, Lightner quit her job and founded Mothers Against Drunk Drivers, or MADD. Completely apolitical until her daughter was killed ("I wasn't even registered to vote"), Lightner began speaking out—using the force of her commitment—before state and federal lawmakers. She enlisted the support of many political leaders and, in six years, turned a one-woman crusade into a 600,000-member organization in forty-seven states.

Her conviction has garnered national publicity and led to several initiatives, including court monitoring and victim outreach programs in local communities. Lightner says, "There are so many people who are worse off than I am—people who have lost two children or their whole family. Nobody cares for them, so it's up to us to be the voice of the victims."

Another person who isn't afraid to show his commitment is Lee Iacocca. He was so committed to turning Chrysler around that when he appealed to Congress for help, they believed him and provided the necessary guarantees the company needed to remain in business. In effect, Congress gave those loan guarantees to Iacocca himself, because they believed in his total devotion to the project.

To repeat, the third essential is *be committed*. What are you committed to? Are you good at showing that commitment to others?

THE FOURTH ESSENTIAL: BE INTERESTING

I meet people every day from every walk of life who are interesting. It's easier than you think to be interesting. It just takes a little imagination and some pluck. For example, a thin, bespectacled, and studious boy went to college, got good grades, and entered the so-called "dismal science" of economics. Today he is one of the most sought-after and interesting speakers on the lecture circuit. He is Milton Friedman, the Nobel Prize–winning economist. Although economics has a reputation for being a dry subject, it didn't make Friedman uninteresting.

At the other end of the spectrum, a mousey girl from a poor family in Tennessee decided that when she grew up she had to be famous. Today, we know her as Dolly Parton. She certainly has a distinctive style—part camp and all "country." Whatever people say about Dolly, she laughs all the way to the bank and jokes, "You'd be surprised how much money it costs to look cheap."

It's difficult to be interesting if you're not committed and vice versa. So these two rules work closely together. No audience (no matter how small or large) will forgive you if you're boring. On the other hand, very few people have ever been fired for giving a boring speech. That's folklore in business. Everybody knows this, so they feel safe in getting up and reading their speeches in a boring way and sitting down. Their audiences are bored, and they all know the speaker is bored. But they feel comfortable with an uninteresting 65 delivery because they know that if everybody's boring, then nobody will stand out. I call this silent collusion the Brotherhood of Boredom. It's one organization you should avoid joining.

STYLE VERSUS SUBSTANCE

Some business speakers will do almost anything to find a way *not* to be interesting. There's a sense among some people in business that style and substance are mutually exclusive. The perception is that if you have style, you must be a lightweight. The same logic says that if you're going to demonstrate substance, you've got to be boring; then the audience will think you're one of the really bright persons who know what they're doing. This is the old way of thinking, and the successful people moving up in the workplace today know it. Don't join the Brotherhood of Boredom—the dues are too high. In today's world it can cost you a promotion.

Here's a perfect example of what I mean. One of my clients was a lawyer in the chemical business. He was a nice guy— one of the smartest I've ever met in the industry—and totally committed to cleaning up the environment. But when he talked about battling pollution, his voice was low and flat. His eyes and face showed no life force. He barely moved his head and shoulders, and his arms hung lifelessly by his sides. There was nothing in his physical expression to convince you that there was urgency in what he was saying.

All of this was bad enough because it showed very little commitment. Even though he said he felt it in his heart, he didn't show it in his body language, or voice, or face. However, even worse, he never said anything interesting about his subject.

I told the client that he was talking much too softly, with too little animation. He needed to raise his energy level. And I asked him what his immediate problems were at work. He said he needed to get a 30 percent increase in the environmental budget from his company, but he didn't think he had the attention of the senior executives, including the CEO. Frankly, I could understand why he didn't have their attention—because of his manner of presentation.

THE FIVE-MINUTE MANAGER

We came up with an exercise which was essentially this: You're going to get five minutes of your chief executive officer's time. Five minutes to get your 30 percent budget increase. You need to demonstrate commitment and be persuasive and get everyone's attention in that short time. You need to sell—not just tell—your point of view.

This is how he did it, after our rehearsal. He walked into a conference room, sat down, leaned forward on the desk, and said in a crisp, clear voice with solid eye contact, "Many companies like ours pay lip service to environmental cleanup. If we make that mistake, it will cost this company one billion dollars over the next seven years." Every executive in that room was riveted. The rest of his presentation was similarly direct. He got the budget increase.

THE BEST AND THE BRIGHTEST

You can have substance in a speech—Winston Churchill did, Franklin Roosevelt did, John Kennedy did—and still have a style of delivery that impresses the audience. It's just plain wrong to think you can't perform well without being shallow or slick. Some of the best speakers in the country are also some of the best thinkers. Notable examples include two retired but still active corporate chairmen—Walter Wriston of Citicorp and

Fletcher Byrom of Koppers. Other examples are Jack Welch of General Electric, Malcolm Forbes, Jr., of *Forbes* magazine, and Tina Brown of *The New Yorker*.

You will be interesting if you do what is called "thinking outside the dots." We all remember that little game of nine dots on a page and having to connect the lines without ever lifting the pencil off the paper. We find that it's impossible to do until we begin drawing the lines longer than the dots allow; in other words, drawing a line outside the dots allows us to be successful.

We must do the same thing when communicating. Don't be limited by the so-called parameters of your subject. Think creatively. Think of analogies from fields that you're not discussing. Think of putting what you're talking about into historical perspective, or comparing it to something which is familiar to your listeners. In other words, just because your topic is the corporation's commitment to environmental safety measures doesn't mean you can't talk about movies, history, people, or ideas which you can somehow relate to your topic.

According to that excellent columnist James Brady, "The legendary book editor Maxwell Perkins—who worked with Ernest Hemingway, F. Scott Fitzgerald, and Thomas Wolfe—was known for always wearing a hat in the office on the theory that, when confronted by a bore, he could escape by saying he was on the way out."[11] If 67 people suddenly throw on their hats when you enter their offices, you might want to start thinking outside the dots more.

Joseph J. Melone, president of The Prudential Insurance Company of America, used an outside-the-dots ending in his remarks at the American College Annual forum in Orlando, Florida, on October 12, 1985:

> Everything I've ever read suggests that those individuals who are most successful in this world—the ones people really look up to—all say the same thing: the greatest joy in life doesn't come from wealth or praise or high honors. It comes from achieving something worthwhile—something of lasting value.
>
> The ancient Romans were noted for their achievements in

construction. Many Roman arches are still standing. They've survived for 2,000 years.

The Romans had an interesting practice. When they finished building an arch, the engineer in charge was expected to stand beneath it when the scaffolding was removed.

If the arch didn't hold, he was the first to know.

Whatever you choose to build with your life, build it so you—and someday your children's children—can stand beneath it with confidence and pride.[12]

THE 30 PERCENT SOLUTION

I often tell my clients they should do at least 30 percent of all their reading outside their own field. This will give them perspective and knowledge that will make them more interesting. Another good practice is to stay in touch with popular culture. For example, flip through *TV Guide, People, Readers Digest,* humourous books or newspaper columns written by people like Russell Baker, Erma Bombeck, and Marvin Kitman, and inflight airline magazines and similar periodicals. Remember or jot down points or stories you can use in conversation and speeches. On an index card you can keep in your wallet, list the key phrases of ten stories that will entertain audiences for the next ten years, because you rarely speak to the same audience twice.

7
THE MAGIC BULLET

If you could master one element of personal communications that is more powerful than anything we've discussed, it is the quality of being *likable*. I call it the magic bullet, because if your audience likes you, they'll forgive just about everything else you do wrong. If they don't like you, you can hit every rule right on target and it doesn't matter.

It's what I call the like factor. In politics, like votes can swing elections. Many elections today are close—53 to 47 percent, for example. Therefore, the number of voters who vote on gut feelings—those who just like one candidate more—is crucial. The same phenomenon exists in business, except that in business, the key votes may be found across the bargaining table with union representatives, or in building relationships between middle managers and their bosses, or in the boardroom when a new CEO is selected.

Corporate or civic leaders who can be tough-minded but likable will be the future's management elite. That's because the leaders of the next ten years will no longer be able to maintain low profiles. They will need to function comfortably in a communications arena very similar to that of today's politicians. The arena will be wide open to public scrutiny and will require winning the goodwill—the like votes—of different constituencies. These include employees, shareholders, government regulators, consumer activists, and—very important—the news media.

Irving Shapiro, former du Pont CEO, said in *Dun's Business Month*, "Above all, the CEO must have the ability to relate to people, both within the organization and outside. He is no longer just running plants and selling goods. Today, he is a quasi-public official, who needs as much skill in dealing with people as any Senator."

A TRICK SHOT

This is a very tricky subject because the magic bullet, *likability*, is difficult to define. Almost no one can tell you exactly how to be likable. People who try too hard to be likable usually aren't. It appears almost as if some people are born likable, and others will never be likable. But in fact, you can do something about your like quotient.

While no one can tell you exactly how to do it, it is possible to define some things that likable people have. It's also helpful to identify unlikable behavior so you can avoid it. People who are unlikable complain about their problems, jabber constantly about meaningless things, and talk in a monotone. They are overly serious and rarely smile or joke about anything. They usually are self-centered.

One quality of likable people is that they are genuinely concerned about the well-being of other people. It's not the phony concern of "How are you today?" and then the blank look while the person answers. A guaranteed way to be unlikable is to talk down to others or to put them down. One of my favorite quotes from Ralph Waldo Emerson is "What you are speaks so loudly, I can't hear what you say."

At least one third of my clients have the problem of being too arrogant or aggressive—either as speakers or as listeners. They turn others off and tune them out because they're overprojecting and underabsorbing. One of the unfortunate byproducts of success often is arrogance.

Perhaps you're sometimes guilty of this, too. Do you say unlikable, put-down phrases like these to others: "You don't understand," "Well, obviously," "Let me start at the beginning,"

"In simple terms," "Let me explain something to you," or "You probably don't know this, but"? If you say these phrases or hear them, you can be sure that a chill will come over the conversation. If you *think* those derogatory thoughts as a listener, you're likewise blocking your ability to hear and understand.

OPTIMISTS AND PESSIMISTS

Another trait of likable people is that they are optimistic. Pessimistic people bring you down; optimistic people bring you up. President Lincoln once said, "The pessimist sees the difficulty in every opportunity and the optimist sees the opportunity in every difficulty." If someone asks you how you are feeling and you actually tell them that things are terrible, people are not going to want to be around you. Extremely shy or depressed people are generally not likable, even though we might feel sympathy for them.

Research by a psychologist at Carnegie-Mellon University in Pittsburgh indicates that optimists handle stress better than pessimists do. Optimists tend to respond to disappointments, like being turned down for a job, by formulating a plan of action and asking other people for help and advice. Pessimists often react to such difficulties by trying to forget the whole thing and assuming there is nothing they can do to change their circumstances. Which kind of person would you rather be around?

Likable people are almost never "poor me," self-pitying people. If you've been around people who always tell you how the world's treating them badly, or how their bosses treat them unfairly, quickly you want to get away. If you want to be likable, avoid being a "poor me" person. Likable people simply lend a hand, have a smile, mind their own business, and laugh easily, especially at themselves. They often understand humor and can get others to laugh.

List five people whom you consider to be unlikable. Then list the characteristics about them that you don't like. Do the same with five people whom you consider to be likable. List their characteristics and why you like them. Study both sets of characteristics. If you emulate the likable people, you will be even more likable yourself. You'll also become a better communicator in the process because you'll carry the magic bullet wherever you go.

AN ALL-TIME FAVORITE

One of my all-time most likable people is Eddy Arnold, the great country music star. Eddy Arnold is one of the top ten record sellers in history, selling over eighty million records to date. In the early 1960s, when I was still a gofer on "The Mike Douglas Show" and had to go to the airport to pick up the stars, my assignment was to pick up Eddy Arnold. At the time, he had two hit records on the charts. After I met him at the airport, we had a pleasant and uneventful ride to the Carter Hotel in Cleveland.

My job was to see that his suite was satisfactory and that he had everything he needed, so that he'd be in a good frame of mind to appear on the show. We picked up his room key at the hotel front desk and proceeded upstairs. When I opened the door to his suite, I was horrified. The room looked as though the boys from Chippendale had spent the weekend with the Dallas Cowboys' cheerleading squad. There were clothes hanging on lamps, furniture upside down, garbage against the walls, and whiskey bottles on the floor. We walked right into this mess. My short career flashed before my eyes.

Very calmly and in his comfortable Tennessee drawl, Eddy Arnold said, "Looks like we've interrupted something here. Maybe we better go have something to eat." So we went downstairs. I told the people at the hotel's front desk what happened. They immediately apologized and said they would get another suite. Eddy took me to dinner.

In my career I've seen many stars throw fits over lesser things. But Eddy just wasn't that kind of guy. The next day at the studio he never said a word to my bosses or to anyone else about the problem we had at the hotel. Because he was so likable that day, Eddy Arnold made a friend for life.

No matter how things are going for you, if you can take the time to realize that somebody else can use a lift, you'll never be forgotten and you'll always be likable.

CHRISTMAS 1965

Years ago, I was working on the East Coast but also producing some television segments on the West Coast for a talk-variety show. Bill Daily was a little-known comedy actor in those days who was involved in the West Coast project. Daily, incidentally, went on to become Larry Hagman's astronaut buddy in the "I Dream of Jeannie" TV series with Barbara Eden. He later played Bob Newhart's neighbor on "The Bob Newhart Show." Daily is one of the funniest men I know.

Back in 1965, at Christmastime, I was working in Philadelphia. There was a crisis in Los Angeles, so I was summoned immediately. I had to leave my family on Christmas Day and go to the airport in a snowstorm. My flight eventually took off but arrived in Los Angeles seven hours late. I got off the plane —rumpled, exhausted, and cranky—at 1:30 A.M. I had been up for twenty-one hours. As I walked down the exit ramp I saw a familiar face in the waiting room. It was Bill Daily.

I couldn't believe my eyes. The airport lounge was practically empty except for Bill. I walked over to him and said, "What the heck are you doing here?"

He just looked at me with a big smile and said, "Ailes, nobody should be alone on Christmas." He reached inside his jacket pulled out a bottle, poured me a drink, and then drove me to the hotel. I've often thought that if people would just go a little out of their way to help others, there'd be no problems with anybody's like quotient.

IT'S NO JOKE

There was a comedian named Shelly Berman who was very popular in the late 1950s and early 1960s. He was filming a television special, and at the time he was considered to be one of the funniest and most successful men in America. People often equate funniness with likability.

A TV crew was recording his routine that night. He was well into his comedy act when a phone rang backstage. The phone interrupted the rhythm of his delivery. He got through that particular story and then walked off the stage.

The camera crew followed him. The phone was still ringing and Shelly Berman grabbed it, screamed into it, and ripped it off the wall. This display of anger and aggression nearly ended his career. His income dropped dramatically by thousands and thousands of dollars. Suddenly one of the funniest men in America was considered unlikable.

A similar incident happened with another comedian of Berman's vintage—Jackie Mason. His career was going brilliantly until one night on "The Ed Sullivan Show," when he allegedly made an obscene hand gesture. Mason's career instantly derailed. He spent years out of the limelight before making a comeback in a 1987 Broadway show. But he admits of the past, "I would say I terribly mismanaged my career." Open displays of ill temper will almost insure unlikability.

THE SPOKESMAN

A few years ago a client called me because the company had agreed to appear on the TV program "20/20." The program's producers wanted someone high up in management to rebut charges that a widely used company product was unsafe. The chairman had identified a few top executives who could speak knowledgeably about the product, and he wanted me to help him select the best spokesperson. After I met with all the candidates, the CEO asked me what I thought of the one he had named as his first choice. I replied that the man knew the subject quite well, but that he came across as rather cold and aloof.

As a TV producer, I had become aware of the importance of not just accurately communicating the facts, but also winning the sympathy of the viewing audience—in effect, winning their like votes. We therefore chose another spokesperson, a down-to-earth, slightly overweight, and avuncular senior scientist. He came into my studio prior to the taping of the show, and we helped him sharpen and edit his delivery. He knew the subject and was committed and interesting. When it came time for his television appearance, he handled himself exceptionally well, despite the aggressive tactics of his interviewer.

His friendly demeanor neutralized a potentially inflammatory attack by "20/20." It also helped diminish possible negative coverage by other journalists who might have followed the program's lead if the story had been hot enough. Incidentally, a few years later, a federal agency declared the product to be safe. But prior to that, one likable, knowledgeable scientist helped to save his company millions of dollars and thousands of jobs—because of his communications skills.

LOSING THE LIKE VOTE

Not only is winning the like vote important with external constituencies such as the press and the general public. It is also a key goal internally with employees. Each year certain magazines like to point out the toughest leaders of corporations. The implication is that with ruthlessness and orneriness they extract the most out of their work forces and fatten the bottom line.

My experience is that, while some of these tough leaders run profitable enterprises, most of them have chronic morale problems. They lose many talented executives, and often they self-destruct because somewhere, somehow, the lack of trust from the troops denies them access to new ideas and the loyalty they need to develop management depth in a competitive world.

I often consult with technically brilliant executives who fail to win support from subordinates and coworkers. They are winners on the academic point scale but losers of like votes, which threatens to torpedo their progress—even their jobs. My job is to give them a candid assessment of how they come across to others, and to counsel them in practical ways to improve their interpersonal relations.

I HATE HIS GUTS

One CEO of a major retailing firm told me he was on the verge of firing a $400,000-a-year executive who was a consistently good bottom-line performer. I was puzzled and asked the CEO why he would fire someone who had performed so well. He said simply, "I hate his guts. Not only that, everybody on the board hates his guts. He has a big mouth and he irritates his peers as well as his superiors. If you can't do anything with him, I'm going to let him go." This was the first time in my experience I had heard that a man doing that well on the bottom line was going to be fired, but I took on the assignment.

I videotaped this executive and involved him in a number of role-playing situations. In effect, I showed him what others saw. Once he had witnessed the hostility and aggressiveness he projected, he was able to move toward a more likable behavior. Three months later, not only had he improved his behavior with his peers in the office, but he was interviewed very favorably by *The Wall Street Journal.*

If you take care of all four essentials well—be prepared, be comfortable, be committed, be interesting—you will be an excellent communicator who never disappoints your audience. But if you can add likability to these four essentials, you will be a master communicator.

8

THE DOUBLE-EDGED SWORD

Emotion is the double-edged sword of communication. When emotion is positive and genuine, there is no more constructive and powerful force of persuasion. But when emotion is negative or insincere, it creates a wall between the person sending the message and those receiving it.

Just consider a few public pronouncements where emotion moved audiences worldwide.

• Martin Luther King, calling for civil rights at the Lincoln Memorial in 1963, declaring, "I have a dream!"

• Astronaut Neil Armstrong, stepping onto the surface of the moon on July 20, 1969, saying, "That's one small step for man, one giant leap for mankind."

• Ted Kennedy, at St. Patrick's Cathedral, June 8, 1968, quoting his assassinated brother Bobby: "Some men see things as they are and say, 'Why?' I dream things that never were and say, 'Why not?' "

• Actress Louise Fletcher, accepting the Academy Award for her portrayal of Nurse Ratched in the film *One Flew over the Cuckoo's Nest*, paying tribute to her deaf parents. With tears rolling down her cheeks, she simultaneously spoke and delivered her message in sign language to her deaf parents watching television at home. She said (and signed), "Thank you for teaching me to have a dream. You are seeing my dream come true."

• General Douglas MacArthur, announcing his retirement before Congress on April 19, 1951. He quoted the popular barracks ballad, saying, "Old soldiers never die; they just fade away." Then he added, "And like the old soldier of that ballad, I now close my military career and just fade away."

• President Franklin Delano Roosevelt, in his 1933 inaugural speech, assuring Depression-wracked America that "the only thing we have to fear is fear itself."

• British Prime Minister Winston Churchill in his speech to the House of Commons in 1940, saying, "Let us therefore brace ourselves to our duties, and so bear ourselves that, if the British Empire and its Commonwealth last for a thousand years, men will still say, 'This was their finest hour.' "

• Prince Edward VIII of Wales, the duke of Windsor, abdicating his claim to the British crown to marry American divorcée Wallis Warfield Simpson by saying, "But you must believe me when I tell you that I have found it impossible to carry the heavy burden of responsibility and to discharge my duties as King as I would wish to do without the help and support of the woman I love."

These were public statements charged with emotion. Recall the impact of some of the emotional communications in your lifetime. Perhaps when your spouse proposed to you. Or when your child said "Mama" or "Dada" for the first time. When you said, "Yes, sir!" (finally loudly enough) to a drill sergeant.

To be a good communicator, you've got to bring some personality and emotion to what you say and how you say it. Whether you're speaking to one or to thousands, you can't just assume the audience is interested only in the words you've written down. If that were the case, you could save yourself a lot of trouble by staying home and just mailing them your speech. Then they could read it on Saturday, when they have more time to concentrate on it.

First and foremost, the audience is interested in you, and that means you've got to put something of yourself on the table. Let your audience know who you are and why you're there. Remember, you are the message. Then you can move into your material.

A RANGE OF EMOTIONS

When the emotions of communication are expressed with commitment and colored by nuance, that is communication at its strongest. The biggest problem many people have with emotion in speaking, however, is that they try to control it or destructively repress it. Often this is where fear takes a grip on them or anger causes them to alienate others. We're all acquainted with the shy person who clams up at a dinner-table discussion or at a business meeting. Or the anxious person at the lectern who stammers because of stage fright.

Too often we hear anger communicated. We hear accusations shouted or sarcasm used. Or, as bad, we hear a tremor in someone's voice caused by ill-concealed rage or frustration or fear. The question is not how we eliminate emotion but, rather, how we use it to our advantage.

People want to see a communicator have a range of emotions. Everybody knew coming out of the Iowa caucuses in 1980 that Ronald Reagan was an affable ex-actor and ex-governor. There was some talk even then that he was too old to really hold down the job, that his mind wasn't sharp enough, and so on. Even his enemies said, "You know, he's a nice fellow." Tip O'Neill said, "I like him." But nobody really felt that he had a range of emotions.

Then, during the New Hampshire primary, just before a debate, the moderator shut off Reagan's microphone. Reagan jumped to his feet, grabbed the microphone, and yelled at the moderator, "I paid for this microphone, Mr. Green." Everybody jumped back and said, "Holy cow, there's more to this guy than we thought. He's capable of getting tough. He's capable of being decisive." That was the turning point of his campaign. That's an example of a person using a range of emotions. And in my opinion, it broadened the concept of Ronald Reagan dramatically.

Many people see the world in one of two ways: They are either emotional or rational. But the world is not that black and white. For years, I've told my political clients that there are heart issues and there are head issues. You can talk about taxes and roads, and those are head issues. They require intellectual conceptualization. But if you start talking about abortion, missing children, or health care, those are heart issues. They concern people.

Martin Luther King's birthday is an emotional issue to many people in this country. You cannot talk about it as a head issue then, because people will think you're cold, insensitive, and even bigoted. People have to feel that you really are sincere, whatever your point of view. If there's no emotion in your communication, they get mixed signals. They know instinctively that the subject is emotional, and they expect to see or feel that you recognize that, too. If they don't, they get this very cold, uncaring feeling about you.

And it's true of CEOs, it's true of television personalities, it's true of anybody. It's true over the back fence to your next-door neighbor. If you come out back and look over the fence and say, "Well, your tomatoes don't look too good this year," that's a negative conversation. If you come out with a smile and say, "Hey, that's great. You're growing tomatoes. I wish I could do that," and smile, you've got a different neighbor. In fact, he's the same neighbor, but you've created a different person by your communication approach.

THE PERSONAL TOUCH

As my associate, Jon Kraushar, says, the facts provide the information and emotion provides the interpretation. You've got to bring something personal to the communication process. Otherwise, you're wasting people's time. You're wasting your own time. To be a really good communicator, you have to start by knowing how you feel personally about what's going on. Then, once you're aware of your own emotions, you can more easily communicate in the right tone to others.

PRESSING TOO HARD

Often in our training we are met with unexpected emotionalism. I'm always glad to see it because I know this person can become a good public speaker. Here's an example of how you can overcome problems in communicating once you come to terms with your feelings.

A client came to me because he suddenly had become terrified of any public speaking situation. It had come on unexpectedly. Prior to that, he had been a pretty good public speaker. Now I'm not a psychiatrist. But I do believe that a lot of problems can be talked out. I tried reviewing with the executive some possible causes for his "blacking out," as he called it. Nothing convincing emerged from our discussion.

I tried to just get him on tape, to get a glimpse, if we could, of his blackout reaction. We wanted to relax him. So we gave him an extemporaneous speaking exercise. We asked him to describe someone unforgettable. He began by talking about a general he had worked for in the Army. Then he mentioned that the general reminded him of his father, and as he began to describe his father, he began to cry.

It turned out his father had recently died. The father had been very tough and demanding during the executive's formative years, pushing the boy to achieve and rarely praising him. Yet, despite some friction between father and son, the son had worshiped his dad.

It all came out in an emotional catharsis during our private session. The executive realized that he was afraid of letting his father down if his speeches weren't excellent. The executive's stage fright turned out to be a temporary paralysis. By simply talking about it, he finally was released from the compulsion to perform up to his father's expectations. This swirl of conflicting emotions apparently had frozen the executive until he came to terms with how he felt.

After a few coaching sessions, the executive's blackouts first diminished, then vanished. He has since received an important promotion and, in fact, has been identified by some leading business magazines as one of the most competent young CEOs in the country—in large part due to his communication skills.

QUALIFICATIONS VERSUS QUALITIES

Emotions affect your overall attitude about life, people, yourself, and your job. When I hire staff for my business, I consider attitude one of the most important job qualifications. In fact, it's not even right to call it a qualification. Many years ago I learned an important lesson from a brilliant television executive named Chet Collier, who was one of the key influences in the development and success of "The Mike Douglas Show." He used to say there are two parts to the job. First, the qualifications you look for. Second, the personal qualities you look for: things like integrity, courage, and hard work. I've never forgotten that, and often the first thing I look for in hiring is the quality of attitude. If the attitude is not right despite all the other qualifications, the person will probably fail.

My work sometimes requires, say, members of my staff to be in several different states on a holiday weekend. The stress on them is tremendous. If we make an error in judgment, we can cost clients millions of dollars and seriously damage their careers. In that high-pressure environment, my staff has to bring others up, not down. They have to solve tough problems while making it look easy and soothe tender egos while driving the team to excel. They must be emotionally well balanced.

Certainly the 1986 insider-trading scandals on Wall Street demonstrated the important link between qualifications and qualities. Each person indicted in the scandal had formidable qualifications—the right schools, the right job achievements, the right industry contacts—but the *wrong* ethics. The qualifications were there. But one of the most important qualities—integrity—was missing.

I've hired hundreds of people over the years for different projects. The resume tells me if the person has qualifications for the job. But what about that person's qualities as a human being? One of the first things I ask when I check someone's references is "How does this person make other people feel?" If I hear on the other end of the phone, "Well, what do you mean 'feel'?" I say, "Do other people like him? Is he trustworthy? Honest? Do others enjoy working with him and being around him?" If I'm told, "He's a real loner, and sort of downcast," I think, "This is probably not going to work."

THE GLASS CEILING

Many women complain that their qualities and qualifications are subject to a double standard in the business world. While the principles in this book apply equally to men and women, I'd like to address the special concerns of women in a few key communications areas. A great many women feel frustrated by male domination in business. Some women, for example, drop out of the corporate rat race because they feel they cannot go all the way to the top. The expression is that an invisible barrier—a "glass ceiling" built by men and society—blocks women from promotion, especially to senior management positions.

Statistics suggest that women are both right and wrong in their allegations. The glass ceiling is often real. But it *can* be penetrated. If nothing else, the sheer logjam of women coalescing nearer to the top has got to create enough pressure for the glass ceiling to crack—if not to break outright. According to *The Wall Street Journal*, in 1982, 21.7 percent of middle management jobs were held by women. In 1992, that figure had risen to 30.5 percent. In 1976, hardly one in eight newly graduated MBAs was a woman. By 1992, that proportion increased to one in three.

Between 1977 and 1994, the number of female directors on the boards of the top five hundred U.S. corporations jumped from 46 to 570—a 1000 percent increase, according to Catalyst, the women's research organization.

Although the representation of women in top management spots remains small overall, the trend lines are set.

AN EVOLUTION

An evolution, rather than a revolution, is taking place. I believe that in ten years we'll see a higher proportion of women in top management spots. Golda Meir once observed that "to be successful, a woman has to be better at her job than a man." By sheer grit and talent, enough women will fight their way through the gauntlet of male chauvinism, family pressures, and corporate political infighting. In ten years there will be more female CEOs and presidents—and not just in publishing and printing, for example, where 8.4 percent of board directors are now women, or in apparel, where 10 percent of corporate officers are women. In ten years there will be women running major high-tech and manufacturing companies, perhaps even a few women at the top of industries like metals and automobiles.

THE HASSLE FACTOR

Women who ultimately succeed in the business world have to rely on their communication skills. It has been my observation that the biggest problems in the workplace occur when what I call the hassle factor comes into play. Women are hassled—stressed, confronted, challenged—in a variety of ways when they come up against mostly male and occasionally certain female negative attitudes in the workplace.

The male hassles may involve men who are blatantly condescending, demeaning, or belittling. These hassles boil down to territorial turf wars. They may be part of the locker-room exclusivity and male bonding of the old-boy network. Men frequently move to the attack too quickly in a hassle in an effort to overpower the woman.

Female-to-female hassles include the difficulties of supervising other women, who occasionally exhibit a sort of reverse chauvinism—they resent female success and authority. Women who hassle other women often fume at their female adversaries, gossiping about them and failing to cooperate with them at a crucial time in the development of a work project.

Regardless of the form of hassle, men often overreact to women when the hassle surfaces. The men yell. They lecture. They whine about the so-called female temperament. They make all kinds of disparaging remarks directly to women—and behind their backs.

Unfortunately, many of the women executives that have come to me for counseling also overreact to all kinds of hassles in one of two ways. The first way is to come on too strong, to become abrasive and think you have to fight fire with fire. That approach just makes for bigger, angrier confrontations. In the second type of reaction, they don't come on strong enough for fear of offending. That doesn't allow the issues in dispute to surface. It only makes frustrations worse.

The best way for a woman to approach confrontations that become tense is to try to *normalize* the situation. Don't give it more importance than it really deserves. Don't back away from it if you need to confront it. But don't feel that as a woman you need to be overly aggressive to be taken seriously. Learn to use neutral language to spell out the situation and how it can be corrected. Once you do that, you'll be standing your ground in a nonthreatening way.

REDIRECTION

Most communications hassles between people in the workplace—whether male or female—amount to a struggle for power: One person wants to one-up the other, so there is a conflict. The secret to overcoming the hassle factor is to *redirect* the negative energy of the conflict into positive energy for you. For example, sociologists Candace West, Donald Zimmerman, and Pamela Fishman, among others, have recorded and analyzed spontaneous conversations between men and women. The patterns that emerged are that many men freely interrupt women and dismiss women's ideas—and many women tolerate this! Instead, women need to firmly but pleasantly wrest back control from men (or women) who try to verbally bully them. The ruses people use to throw women off track vary widely. Sometimes it's a diversionary tactic, such as a man's interrupting a woman who is running a meeting by saying, "You've got the most gorgeous eyes" or a similar comment about her looks or dress. Or it may be an annoying dig at the woman's authority. Sometimes patronizing phrases are used, such as ". . . well, of course, you don't have the experience, but . . ." or ". . . I know this will be hard for you to understand, but . . ."

Women faced with these and other forms of communication sabotage should counter in an active yet friendly manner by saying, "Excuse me, but . . ." or a similar phrase to minimize the distraction and *redirect* the discussion back to the business at hand. Your goal is to gently regain control without hostility, confrontation, or impingement on the sensitive egos of the people involved. You'll recover the authority that someone else tried to usurp from you and prevent that person from "delegitimizing" you.

SOME ADVICE

Based on experiences of women I know and work with, I'll make two definite statements. First, women are generally better communicators than men because they absorb more quickly and often read the emotions of the situation as well as the facts. With these skills, their "radar" can locate the neutral zone where a confrontation should be moved to normalize the conflict. Second, my advice to women is to be true to the best aspects of being feminine. A woman who acts like a man in the workplace is as silly as a man who acts like a woman in the workplace. Many women have felt, with some justification, that if they didn't toughen up and act macho and be one of the boys, they would never get along. Women: Stay true to your identity. Whatever you do, keep in mind that, as in all communications, your tone of voice, the expression in your eyes, the attitudes conveyed by your face and body will determine how others interpret your words. And above all, keep your sense of humor and your sense of perspective.

"BILINGUAL" COMMUNICATIONS

Some of the best thinking I've seen on men and women in the workplace has been done by Susan E. Davis, a vice president of Harris Trust and Savings Bank in Chicago. In a speech at Ripon College on April 4, 1985, Davis said, "I have a simple thesis that it is the manager who is 'bilingual' who will be the successful manager of the eighties. By 'bilingual,' I mean someone who is comfortable with and adept at using the cultural values and styles of both men and women." Davis went on to say that to be bilingual, men need to become more comfortable with more communication, and women with less communication. Men need to become more comfortable with decision making by consensus, women with unilateral decision making. Men need to become more comfortable with sharing responsibility, women with delegating responsibility. Men need to become more comfortable with corporate social responsibility, women with profit responsibility. Men need to become more comfortable with taking a long-term view, women with taking a short-term view. Men need to become more comfortable with less (blind) loyalty to superiors, women with more (consistent) loyalty to superiors. Men need to become more comfortable with acting on feelings, women with acting on ideas. And finally, men need to become more comfortable with appreciating gossip (legitimate complaints), and women with depreciating gossip (idle chatter).

Whether you're male or female, go back over this list and evaluate yourself on its criteria. Are you overemphasizing—or underemphasizing—any of the qualities listed? Would your boss and/or coworkers see you as you see yourself? Do some hard thinking about this, because Davis has identified some of the qualities that can make or break your career. In my judgment, one of the most important qualities for success in the workplace is a good attitude.

MEASURE YOUR ATTITUDE

Here are excerpts from a self-assessment quiz relating to attitude that I've given to my staff. Score yourself from one ("I'm not good at this") to five ("I'm outstanding at this").

1. How good are you at confronting other people directly when there is a problem, without biasing the confrontation in a negative manner?

2. How often do you give excuses for things that go wrong? Do you pass the buck or blame others?

3. Are you a self-starter? Are you too passive or are you an active self-starter every day?

4. Do you gossip, spread rumors, or create problems among the work force?

5. How well do you communicate with your fellow employees, both in giving information and in receiving information?

6. How are you at teamwork, helping others, pitching in, and supporting the staff?

7. Are you a person who brings other people up or drags them down emotionally? What is your general enthusiasm level?

8. Do you accept criticism gracefully—neither overreacting or underreacting, but using the best of it to improve?

As with our other self-assessments, consider asking a friend, coworker, or boss to score you. The top score is forty. If you scored thirty-six or more, either you are a near perfect superstar or you might consider asking a couple of other coworkers to score you to see if they agree. Few people are consistently in this category. If you're in the twenty-five to thirty-five range, you are above normal—doing a good job—but have some room for improvement. If you scored eighteen to twenty-four, you'd better start improving your attitude immediately. If your score is seventeen or less, no matter how well you're doing in the other areas of your job, you're in danger of being fired. You'll need to improve your attitude dramatically—and quickly.

The qualities of emotional balance and a good attitude are as important to you as gas and oil are to your car. If a tune-up (or overhaul) is called for, get right on it.

9

BEYOND CHARISMA: CONTROL OF THE ATMOSPHERE

"Charisma" is a powerful but often misunderstood word. It derives from the Greek *kharisma*, meaning favor or divine gift, and its root is *kharis*, meaning grace. In politics, the idea of charisma came into play a quarter of a century ago, when Jack Kennedy burst upon the American political scene as a presidential candidate. It's really an old-fashioned word now—it's like "gee whiz." Charisma had to do with a look and a style, and today we expect more than that.

Every leader wants to have "charisma" in its modern sense, which the dictionary defines as "a special, inspiring quality of leadership." Some people seem to have charisma naturally; others work hard to achieve it. Some have it in person but lose it on television.

Charisma is *personal* confidence as opposed to *job* confidence—just the sense that someone knows what he or she is doing. Charisma is comfort. It's the ability to never appear uncomfortable.

Some people define charisma as sex appeal. Some see it as an almost electric vigor or vitality. Some see it as authority. It includes all of these ingredients, but it's more. It's really the ability to subtly cause others to react to *you* as opposed to your reacting to them. People with charisma seem to be in charge of their lives. They seem to have a goal, a purpose, a direction—in fact, a mission.

If you're famous, you have a kind of automatic charisma. Just think of Robert Redford or Oprah Winfrey. But I've also seen charismatic people who are not well-known personalities walk into a room and take charge. Sometimes they use silence, sometimes they use humor. But they cause everybody else in the room to respond to them in a positive way.

HAVE YOU GOT IT?

People who are not necessarily stars can be charismatic. I recall a charismatic cop I met when I was directing a commercial in California. It was a tough law-and-order commercial and we needed a policeman to do it. But we also needed a policeman who could read the TelePrompTer, move well, and take action cues. His job was to come through a dark alley, walk up to a police car with a red light shining on top, lean into the camera, and deliver the entire commercial in twenty-six seconds. That's a fairly complicated set of directions for a nonprofessional. After a casting search, I was asked to see a man named Jack Hoar. He was a Los Angeles undercover cop who also had done some small movie roles, most notably a tough guy in the film *To Live and Die in L.A.* Casting on this particular job was critical because even if the performer could do all of the mechanical things correctly, the audience absolutely had to believe his confidence, commitment, and credibility.

After meeting Jack, I hired him without even giving him a test reading. I just knew he could do it. He had charisma. His eyes and voice never wavered. When I asked him if he thought he could do it, he didn't do an "aw shucks" and look away and say, "I hope so." He simply looked at me and quietly said, "Yes, I can do it." We shot one night in an alley in Sacramento. After taking three hours to set the camera track and lights, water down the alley, and line up the camera angles, I called for Jack to come onto the set. He's six feet three inches, 220 pounds, and all muscle from the neck down, brains from the neck up. He did exactly what we needed. He delivered his lines perfectly on the first take.

However, when you shoot a commercial, you often do what are called safety takes. These are reshoots of the commercial so that when you get in the editing room, you have a choice to cover for a technical problem you may have missed when you were shooting. For example, sometimes cars would go through the shot at the end of the alley where we worked. Or there would be ambient noise on the microphone. Perhaps the camera wouldn't be precisely focused. Often, when you cue an actor to repeat his performance over and over again, he begins to lose confidence and thus lose that commitment and charisma you need on the screen. Jack never did. He was as steady on take eighteen as he was on take one. We finally produced an excellent commercial. He had the kind of charisma that was not loud or flashy, but whenever he spoke, everyone on the crew listened and answered him with respect.

To determine whether or not you have the ingredients to be charismatic, answer the following questions: What are your real feelings about who you are? What do you believe in? Do you have goals or a mission in life? Do you project optimism? Do others turn to you for leadership? Noncharismatic people spend their lives auditioning for others and hoping they'll be accepted. Charismatic people don't doubt their ability to add value to a situation, so they move forward with their mission.

Former Treasury Secretary and Texas Governor John Connally had a great deal of personal charisma. When you were in a room with him, you just felt that he was in charge. I even saw him arrive late for a meeting with cabinet officials and the president. All activity stopped while everyone watched Connally walk all the way around an enormous conference table and sit down. Then the meeting resumed. These were all important people and they stopped for him because he was that imposing. He just moved with that kind of confidence. Very few people have that much presence, but he was one of them. He *looked* in charge.

Connally's flaw was that he sometimes came across as arrogant and a little pompous. Those qualities are magnified on a television screen. That's one of the reasons he never became president.

LBJ

Lyndon Johnson couldn't translate his earthy, good-old-boy charisma to television, either. But in a room with three or four other people, he had tremendous charisma. In person, Johnson was a larger-than-life character—gruff, coarse, raw-humored, intimidating, and yet magnetic. He just overpowered you. But when he faced the nation on television, he underwent a personality transformation. He became stiff. He attempted to look serious, dignified, and presidential, largely because television was one of the few things that managed to intimidate *him*. He was afraid that the news media and intellectuals would watch him up close and brand him a hopeless cornpone. The irony is that they did anyway. Johnson should have just skipped the raw language and otherwise been himself on TV. But he always seemed to be auditioning for the public on television instead of letting the medium adapt to him.

THE KENNEDY BROTHERS

Charisma came easily to John Kennedy. With his good looks, his background, his money, he had style and easy grace. But his brother Bobby didn't have the same charm—at least not on the day I met him. I went to Washington to film Robert Kennedy in his office for a television special that we were doing for Westinghouse Broadcasting. He had a high, thin voice and he sat on the edge of his desk, almost in the fetal position. We had tremendous difficulty getting him to use eye contact or gestures at all. I don't think I've ever been around anyone who was quite as uptight. Now this was sometime after his brother had been killed, probably 1964. He was very polite and answered all the questions, but he could not maintain eye contact or project his voice very well. It was interesting for me to see him later run for president. Somewhere along the way, he must have gained confidence, or else he'd had an off day on the occasion we'd met. More likely, as a presidential candidate he was imbued with a sense of mission—a goal—and many of his communications problems cleared up automatically.

FROM HERE TO ETERNITY

Hubert Humphrey's one-on-one charisma gave him an amazing ability to work a crowd. I watched him on a street in Philadelphia one day. In a split second, he was able to give everyone he met the impression that he was interested and concerned for them as individuals. He could just touch someone's hand and use his eyes to make it work. He connected with every person, even though he was moving rapidly toward his car. He imparted a feeling of warmth, so it was impossible to dislike the man. On a personal basis, Humphrey was one of the warmest, nicest people I've ever met.

But he, like LBJ, was never able to translate that to television. I once saw him on a talk show. The host asked Humphrey a question and he gave an *eleven*-minute answer. He just kept talking, and they couldn't even interrupt him to go to a commercial. Finally, the host started looking off-camera, as if to say, "What the hell did I ask? I don't know how to get out of this." Humphrey never understood that television is a time-sensitive medium, and he was never able to get to the point quickly. When he gave a speech on television he strained his voice, and this gave him a strident, high-pitched quality. When he was angry, he sounded whiney instead of tough.

His wife, Muriel, on the other hand, had more charisma than her husband, because she was completely comfortable on television. She was aware of everything and everyone around her. She was just natural without a bit of pretense about her.

ROCKY'S PUNCH

Nelson Rockefeller was the same way. Although he was extremely wealthy, Rocky loved to tell people that he went to public school in New York City up near Harlem, and that he used to roller-skate to school with his friends. Of course, what he never mentioned was that there was a limousine following behind with bodyguards, and when he and his friends got tired, they got into the limo. But he was great at telling that kind of story and carrying it off.

Nelson could never remember anybody's name, so everybody was "Hiya, fella, how's it goin'?" He was very physical. He would touch people, grab the workers' hands, and look at people directly. Even with the Rockefeller name, wealth, and power, he was able to project himself as "one of the guys." He left a strong personal impression, and I believe that had a lot to do with his charisma.

THE GAUNTLET

It's tougher today to be viewed as charismatic. In the heyday of the people just mentioned, the press was not nearly as diligent as it is now in finding and exposing weaknesses in public figures. In fact, many of the faults of these charismatic people didn't come out until after their deaths. To be considered charismatic on a national—or even local—scale today, you have to run a media gauntlet for a number of years and not allow the reporters to find a skeleton in your closet that can bring you down. Despite this relentless scrutiny, there are still people today whom the public respects and looks up to—people with personal charm who someday may be viewed as charismatic figures.

In popular culture, those who have charisma include John Madden, former coach of the Oakland Raiders football team, who has become a funny, hip, and dynamic television sports commentator. Golfer Lee Trevino is charismatic. He seems comfortable with himself, confident, and likable. Legendary golfer Arnold Palmer has charisma, too, because he's the grand old man of the sport—and he's still playing. The longevity of his appeal is notable in our times, when many celebrities rise like comets one month and then fall like shooting stars the next. Palmer is viewed as a man who has lived his life in the way he wanted to live it. That's the dream of many.

Anatoly (Natan) Sharansky, the Russian Jewish dissident who was finally released after several years in Soviet prisons, is viewed as a hero—a man tempered by the fire of mistreatment, yet good-humored and free-spirited throughout his ordeals. For example, when the Russians released Sharansky, they ordered him to walk perfectly straight across a bridge to his freedom. But in an act of whimsical defiance, he zigzagged in almost Chaplinesque fashion across the bridge. In a pantomime captured by news photographers and understood around the world, Sharansky *communicated* the truth of the saying that "you have not converted a man because you have silenced him."

Chuck Yeager has the charisma of an authentic American hero. He flew the X-1 jet, he was nearly killed several times as a test pilot, and he came through World War II as a fighter ace. He's cool, confident, and unflappable, and he has a good sense of humor. He's a man who has looked death in the eye and won. People admire that.

Authentic charisma usually requires a lifetime of achievement. Sometimes intense and dramatic events like wars or hijackings provide the circumstances that can give people charisma. For a short time, the inner strengths of a few protagonists are exposed in the public arena. Some people display courage, leadership, faith. These are attributes that can make people charismatic, whether they're found on the battlefield or in the boardroom.

YOUR CHARISMA QUOTIENT

To summarize, you can measure the degree to which you are charismatic by rating yourself on the following qualities, scoring yourself from a minimum of one ("Not true of me at all") in ascending numbers to a maximum of five ("Describes me exactly"):

- Self-confident (in myself, as opposed to confidence related to my job or material possessions)
- Comfortable with myself
- Able to make others comfortable
- In charge of my life
- Having concrete goals and a definable mission (sense of purpose)
- Seen by others as a leader
- Natural and unpretentious, regardless of circumstances

Add your score up and divide by seven. If your average score is one to two, you need to take stock of yourself. You're very low overall in charisma. You should think about why you rated yourself as you did and discuss it with a friend or even your boss. Based on suggestions in this book, try to develop an action plan to enhance your personal dynamism.

If your average score is three to four, you have a good charisma quotient. But try formulating a personal action plan, because everyone can improve.

That same advice goes to the few people who average five on this self-evaluation. Those who are very charismatic need the stimulation of challenge. Write down ways you can harness your charisma—new relationships, projects, and goals.

CONTROL OF THE ATMOSPHERE

Regardless of how you scored in the charisma self-evaluation, I feel it's important that a person use the elements of charisma but move beyond them to something I call control of the atmosphere. Control of the atmosphere is control of the time and space you work in. When you control the atmosphere, you're not operating on other people's time. You set your own rate of speed for saying things. You pause and pace your rate of speaking for maximum impact. You have no fear of silence. You're not reacting to and feeling inhibited by physical space or people. You use gestures; you move effectively, assertively, when and how you please—whether behind a lectern or on the factory floor. You use your eyes, you show a range of emotions, and you modulate your voice with purpose—not like a shotgun scattered all over the room. You look directly into people's eyes, and you use your voice and eyes like a rifle. In a room of thirty, or fifty, or even a hundred people, you pick out anyone you want to talk to and, boom, you can direct your voice and your eyes to them. Vocally and with your eyes you can express a range of emotions, including amusement, excitement, and even anger, where appropriate. All these abilities are included in control of the atmosphere.

MISSION CONTROL

You *can* learn to control the time and space you move through, if you really believe in yourself and understand what your mission is in every situation. It helps if you look a certain way, but that doesn't mean you have to be handsome or beautiful. In fact, many charismatic people do not look as though they'd been stamped out by a cookie cutter. For example, the ascetic-looking Mahatma Gandhi was charismatic. Winston Churchill with his squat, bulldog countenance and trademark cigar was charismatic. Anwar Sadat's rugged face and proud bearing were charismatic.

In popular culture today, Bruce Willis, star of the *Die Hard* movie series, has potential charisma. There's a certain cockiness about him, but an enormous likability. He appears to be Peck's bad boy with a good heart. If he maintains some humility and doesn't start believing his own press releases, he can go on to become a long-term charismatic actor. Tom Selleck is not a great actor. He's a competent actor with terrific looks, but that is not the secret to his charisma. The secret is that while he is very handsome, men are not threatened by him—they like him. Women, of course, are attracted to him and like him. But he appears to have a gentle soul in an enormously masculine body and face. He's unthreatening and he looks kind. That combination makes him charismatic.

Keep in mind that charisma is not as simple as a look or style. It is frequently a combination of elements which make you different in the eyes of people you meet. You must have your own style. You *do* have to look strong, confident, grounded, and happy with yourself. You must convey your thoughts and show your feelings with conviction. Humor helps, of course. The ability to not always respond in a predictable manner helps, too. But all this means taking risks, and a lot of people don't want to do that.

If you're properly controlling the atmosphere, you're projecting a likable fearlessness—without arrogance. The ability to do that consistently will take you beyond charisma.

The natural reaction of most people when they encounter a new situation is to find out what's going on in the room and try to become invisible, to avoid changing or interrupting it. If you're prepared to go into any kind of communication process and *change* the flow, you have the opportunity to take control of the atmosphere.

RISK AND REWARD

All of this requires risk. You have to be able to speak up at certain times and move the direction of your thoughts *to* other people, cause them to react to you for whatever reason. When you do this, however, it must impress the others as being appropriate, relevant, useful, and interesting. Don't speak up to hear yourself talk or just to insert your opinion. People will turn off.

Some people try to control others by dominating the conversation, talking too slowly, repeating themselves, or using other manipulative techniques, such as showing annoyance at interruptions or refusing to relinquish the floor. That is control in a negative sense and not to be confused with control of the atmosphere.

Control of the atmosphere does not necessarily mean that

you do all the talking. In fact, if you learn to ask interesting questions, you can control the topics which are discussed while at the same time opening up the listener and allowing him or her to communicate with you.

BAR NONE

Eavesdrop at the bar of any night spot that is popular with single people. You'll see and hear the difference between control and control of the atmosphere. Off in the corner you may spot a handsome young man who may be alone—relaxed and quiet—or with friends in easy, lighthearted conversation. He is controlling the atmosphere. Some of the women hoping to meet a nice fellow are probably glancing at him. At some point, another handsome young man will come up to the bar. But he'll try to control the introduction between himself and a young lady. With a cocky air and an arrogant tone of voice, he might use one of those opening lines which young women have told me they've heard: "Are you as good as you look?" or "You've got thirty seconds to convince me to stay here."

People who struggle to control the atmosphere like that never can, much as people who work too hard at trying to be likable usually aren't. The line of demarcation involves the balance between how you absorb and how you project. If that can sometimes be unclear for you, try this approach: Almost everybody likes a person who is sincerely interested in them and does not dominate the conversation, so start there. A *Washington Post* reporter once told me that the first time she interviewed Henry Kissinger, he thoroughly disarmed her by smiling warmly and saying, "Before we get to me, why don't you tell me about yourself?"

DEPTH CHARGES

Among many young executives, there is confusion about the use of control in communication. There is a dark side to the very real achievements of some of the young urban professionals or "yuppies" who make up much of the up-and-coming executive corps today. The complaint I hear most often from older executives is that a number of the younger people—particularly the MBAs from the top business schools—are brilliant but smug. They are knowledgeable but are often glib and arrogant. "What's missing when they communicate with you," says one of my clients, "is the depth which experience brings to the facts. No one expects young people to be anointed with that special depth at such an early age—but many of them act as if they have it. They lecture you like you're an idiot."

Another client told me, "Some of the whiz kids come across as hard—but without density. Once you get past their analytical, numbers-crunching pyrotechnics and surface bravado, you often find they're bright but shallow. If they don't improve their people skills, they're going to spend their careers alienating others—with disastrous results. The pity is, many of them never understand—or admit—that their insensitive style of communicating is the problem."

This obviously isn't true of all ambitious young people. The classic clash between young and old has gone on for centuries, but I am hearing a growing number of complaints like the ones just mentioned. If you know someone who fits the description, perhaps it's time for a friendly chat to cool him down.

It can be a subtle process to communicate effectively when you're a junior person in the same room with senior executives, but it can be done. If you do it in a way that doesn't offend your superiors, you will eventually become a senior person. That's the trick. A lot of it gets back to how people feel about you. They have to be comfortable with you. If you have any doubt about how comfortable you make others feel, be sure to take the self-assessment test at the end of this chapter.

CLIMATE CONTROL

Let me describe a situation where it's the senior person who is in poor control of the atmosphere. Imagine that a boss walks into a conference room. He's got a frown on his face. The staff

sits at attention. The boss, visibly irritated, sits down and demands, "Give me the report from St. Louis." The whole room
is tense. This may be appropriate on occasion. But if he comes
in and puts others at ease with a few casual comments or
questions, he creates a more comfortable climate and people
will respond more openly. That's really "you are the message"
in its simplest form. According to motivational speaker Zig Zig-
lar, winners are thermostats—they set the right temperature.
Losers are thermometers—they go up and down according to
conditions they think are outside of their influence.

UNSPOKEN GIVEAWAYS

With many people who don't control the atmosphere, you notice it first nonverbally. They stand up to address a business
meeting, and their shoulders hunch and their eyes shift. They
look in one of three directions: at the floor, as if hoping an
escape hatch will open and swallow them; at the nearest exit,
as if wishing to get out fast; or at the ceiling, as if praying for
divine guidance. What interferes with the comfortable use of
their body is that they become self-conscious because the atmosphere has changed. Originally a part of the group, they've
separated—physically—and they feel exposed and vulnerable.
People who control the atmosphere recognize that moving
away from the group actually puts you in a position of leadership. Others are following your moves.

SPACE AND TIME

Good communicators control space. It takes time to get control.
If you stand up to speak to a group at a meeting, move to the
front of the room confidently. Take the home base position,
which is with feet balanced about six inches apart. If there is
a lectern, rest your hands comfortably on each side of it. Look
directly at your audience, and then take a second longer than
you think you should to start. Smile as you begin. Remember,

smiling is in the brain, not in the facial muscles. Gesture freely, spontaneously, and fully, without planning to "move your arms." Gesture above the waist so your audience can see your physical expressiveness. Return to home base between gestures. Speak with feeling, from your heart as well as your head. Use a conversational style. Above all, you must believe what you are saying. That's controlling the atmosphere.

Good speakers control their rate of speech because they're comfortable with silence. Most of us are not. We feel pressure to say things as quickly as we can, or we have a rigid, sloweddown process of thinking things through so we don't make a mistake. Those are two common extremes, and the result is someone who speaks too quickly or someone who speaks too slowly. In fact, free-form phrasing is preferable. Audiences don't mind watching you think on your feet, as long as you signal that you're in control of your time and space.

John Wayne had a great film presence, in part, because of the way he controlled the rate of his speech (time). The Duke described his trademark speech pattern this way: "I cut each sentence in half. I say the first half, stop, then say the second half." Movie buffs will recall specific lines where that distinctive rhythm helped make Wayne's delivery so memorable. The point, though, is for all of us to be aware that time (rate of speech, pausing, silence) can be used dynamically when we communicate.

PLAYING FOR TIME

Here's a trick I sometimes use when I give a speech. Someone introduces me and I move to the lectern. There's a definite time when I should begin speaking. I take one extra beat before beginning. Now the individuals in front of me become an audience because they all are focused on the same thing: When is this guy going to say something? Most speakers rush to the lectern, rustle around with their papers, and never take control of the time or space. They mumble under their breath, "Good evening, it's nice to be here," and they never look at their audience. Or they glance up and then right back down to read an introduction. They're off to a weak and stumbling start.

SOCIAL SECURITY

People who control the atmosphere don't change according to who's in the room. They are aware of the interests of the audience. But if they're at Windsor Castle, they don't grovel before the queen, nor do they talk down to the gardener or shoeshine man. They act comfortably, pretty much the way they would in the living room, no matter who they're with.

You can always tell if people are comfortable with their situation and with who they are by noting whether or not they try to adapt to each person in the room according to his or her social station. People who control the atmosphere don't act threatened, frightened, or superior. They treat everybody with the same comfort level and the same goodwill.

Betty White, star of the "Golden Girls" television program, is one of the nicest people in show business. She's a very private person with a great sense of humor. Essentially she is a very kind, intelligent woman. I first met her twenty-five years ago. She treated everyone—whether it was the prop boy or the executive producers—with the same openness and friendliness. There was never any distinction because somebody was powerful. When I first met her, I was the gofer for "The Mike Douglas Show." Many stars walked in and gave me orders, like "Get me a cup of coffee." They reserved their smiles for the more important people. But Betty White took as much time to talk to me as she did to anybody else. A few years later I became a producer, and often when we needed a guest on the show, I'd ask, "Is Betty White available?"

PULLBACK GESTURES

It's also important to have an air of certainty about you in order to control the atmosphere. Use graceful gestures that are in sync with what you're saying, and move in a gliding motion, rather than clumsily or self-consciously. FDR had great control of the atmosphere, even though he was confined to a wheelchair.

I believe the way you move has to do with confidence and an inner sense of yourself. For instance, watch people gesture in meetings. Some will make weak or halfhearted gestures, or what I call pullback gestures. They half raise their hand and then pull it back, or they'll weakly wave a limp hand or finger to get attention. When I see someone move forward with a gesture and then pull it back quickly, that signals to me that this is not a confident person. It's a subconscious signal to others, and it can kill your control of the atmosphere.

HAIL AND WELL MEANT

If you're committed to what you're saying, you don't pull back halfway. It's like hailing a taxi in New York City. I once heard a woman say that she could tell whether or not she wanted to have a second date with a man by the way he hailed a taxi in New York. This is one instance where there is no way to be too aggressive. She said she once went out with a man who, when he saw a cab, raised his hand weakly and quickly, then pulled it right back, saying, "Taxi?" in a tentative voice. After five or six cabs went by, she pushed him out of the way, moved into the middle of the street, shouted, whistled, flagged down a cab, opened the door, and threw the man in. But that was the last time she ever went out with him. In New York, there's only one way to do it. You put your hand up forcefully, wave, and yell, "Taxi!"

We often see someone hesitantly raise a hand, then pull it back. We see people start to speak up and then trail off, or muffle their voices with their hands in front of their faces. That kills the command presence which is part of controlling the atmosphere. Nobody's going to follow a tentative person. You can be calm, cautious, and deliberate, but *not* tentative. There's a certainty to people who control the atmosphere. Whether they're right or wrong, at least they're certain; so people follow them. I wouldn't say it's essential to move like a boxer or a dancer, but it doesn't hurt to have that kind of grace. In any case, when you do move, do it with certainty.

The same thing is true of the eyes, by the way. There are people who will start by saying something very strong and looking right at you, but three words into the sentence, they break eye contact and look at their shoes or out the window. In a tough negotiation, I watch that very carefully. If the other guy can keep looking right at me as he sells his point of view, I know he's committed to it. He may be right or wrong, but I know he's someone I have to deal with. He's formidable. If somebody starts off very aggressively and then backs off with his eye contact or body language, I know I've got room to move, to be aggressive myself.

TEST OF STRENGTH

So the first part of eliminating uncertainty is to be aware of your feelings. Do I feel strongly about this? Why am I intimidated? Watch yourself on videotape and determine the following: Do I use pullback gestures? Do I lose eye contact in the middle of sentences although I want people to believe I'm committed to what I'm saying? If these are true, then you don't have control of the atmosphere. Practice maintaining eye contact under stress. Be cool under fire. Practice making your gestures in one direction and holding them, then releasing them gently.

I can always tell the ones who treat their eye contact and smiles as a form of gamesmanship, because they're always beaming at me bright-eyed with toothy, pasted-on grins. Somebody told them they should have this very penetrating eye contact, and that's as wearing as talking with somebody who doesn't look at you at all. At yuppie cocktail parties, I always catch these young, up-and-coming executives running around giving bone-crushing handshakes while grinning and locking eyes with me. The type of eye contact that's best is gentle and comfortable, not one that feels forced.

CONTROL-OF-THE-ATMOSPHERE QUOTIENT

Let's step back, as we did before, to take a personal inventory of what it takes to go beyond charisma. Score yourself on your ability to control the atmosphere, from one ("Not true of me at all") up to five ("Describes me exactly").

When I speak to others, I am always in control of:

- Time (rate of speech, pauses)
- Space (where and how I move)
- Eye contact (not just where I look and at whom, but the emotional messages my eyes send)
- My voice volume, pronunciation, changes in pitch, and tone)
- My state of mind (calm, happy, upbeat, self-confident)
- My attitude (unthreatened, open-minded, friendly)
- The flow of dialogue (I know when and how to insert my ideas and opinions)
- The absorb-project balance
- My feelings (I admit them to myself, understand them, and communicate accordingly)

There are nine questions and a possible forty-five-point perfect score. If you score over thirty-five on this test, you're doing an excellent job of controlling the atmosphere. A score of twenty-nine to thirty-five, means you're good. The range of twenty to twenty-eight is average. And below twenty, you are failing at this very important aspect of communications. In our next chapter, we'll examine the quality that can turn a good communicator into a great one.

10
AN OUNCE OF ENERGY IS WORTH A POUND OF TECHNIQUE

I can correct fifteen communication technique problems with one ounce of energy. It's so fundamental to success. Of course, that doesn't mean that you come on like some used-car salesmen, leaping all over people, because that really turns everybody off. With the right kind of energy, you're absorbing what others are broadcasting to you. You project enthusiasm, and most so-called speech problems clear up automatically. A good communicator's energy is perceived as "life force," vitality—an aliveness and vigor exemplified at its best by very good communicators like John F. Kennedy, Lee Iacocca, Elizabeth Dole, the young Muhammad Ali, Ted Koppel, and Barbara Walters. One of the absolute rules for control of the atmosphere is focused energy. Many people have trouble focusing their energy in formal presentations like speeches. Either they are too inhibited to let themselves go, or they overdo it.

FOCUSED ENERGY

Properly focused energy comes across as positive, a magnetic intensity, rather than negative, an overwrought intensity. It is an inner flame that we all display when we sincerely believe something and we talk about it. We're committed. Intuitively we know true energy when we see and hear it in a communicator. It is the energy associated in its most consistent form with Harry Truman, Martin Luther King, and Winston Churchill. We all have known people who radiate this "life force" in abundance. Maybe it's a parent, a friend, a coach, a teacher, or a member of the clergy. When people with energy speak, or even listen, they don't display inattention, lack of focus in the eyes, or lack of interest on the face. People in love have energy. People who truly relish their jobs have energy. Communicators with positive energy are involved with their audience (whether one or a thousand) and their message. Because they believe in what they're saying, you believe them. You may disagree with them, but you can't question their conviction. Keep this rule in mind: If you have no energy, you have no audience.

A NATURAL STATE

If your energy is up, your rate, volume, and pitch will be appropriate to the communications situation. If you are enthusiastic, if your posture is good, if you're friendly, and if you're comfortable, you have the "right" kind of energy. Here's the good news: We have all demonstrated energy at some time in our lives. At those times, we've been excellent communicators. It is a completely natural state. Remember back to a moment when you know you were communicating effectively because you absolutely believed in what you were saying. Remember how you felt? Harness that power and you will be successful at communications.

When I first started speech coaching I did it the old-fashioned way: with drills and practice on rate, pitch, and volume. My clients made progress, but it was slow and tedious. Today, I do it organically. I work on the energy level of the communicator. Is it appropriate for the situation? What are his goals? What is he trying to say? What does he mean? How does he feel? How much does he care? If he is in touch with these things, his technique will improve quickly and, often, dramatically. Instead of trying to remember several speech variables—like pitch, rate, volume, and gestures—just remember "energy" and all the variables will take care of themselves. I put the letter E in the margin of all my speeches to remind me of energy.

Today, tomorrow, or next week, when you experience strong feelings and high energy, make a mental note of what you're thinking about. It will be something about which you feel strongly. My experience is that just about everyone gets good at communications when they get emotional. I don't mean "out of control" emotional—that's overly energetic; that's unfocused energy. We've all seen high-strung people or people who flap around, overgesturing. That's negative energy—motion in search of purpose.

POSITIVE ENERGY

How do you get that kind of positive energy, especially when you're nervous about giving a speech, chairing a meeting, or being interviewed for a job or by the news media, for example?

Ask yourself: What am I thinking about? Am I focused on positive things like "This is an opportunity. . . . Let me review my agenda: What are the points I want to make? This can be fun; I've been asked to speak because they believe I'm an authority and can contribute something"? These kind of thoughts will energize you in a way that will help you be successful. The reverse is also true. Negative thoughts can energize you. But they won't help you. Examples of negative thoughts are "What if I go blank? I'll make a mistake and my boss will fire me. I'd rather be anywhere but here." Negative thoughts create self-destructive energy. As Elbert Hubbard said, "The greatest mistake you can make in life is to be continually fearing you will make one."

You don't have to go through life demonstrating energy. But there are certain times, such as when you make a presentation, that you need to marshal your positive energy.

JACK BENNY'S SECRET

One of America's greatest comedians, Jack Benny, taught me about energy. Benny was one of my heroes because he was able to get a laugh just by walking on stage. His timing was perfect. His facial expression was unsurpassed. He was not just a comedian, but also a great comic actor. His strength was not so much in telling jokes as in getting laughs within the parameters of the script, such as a comedy sketch. In over fifty years in show business, he never did anything that was off-color, but he always entertained the audience. Late in his career, when he was quite old, Jack was a guest on "The Mike Douglas Show."

When my assistant told me he was waiting in my office, I rushed in to meet the great man. I found instead a frail little old man hunched over in a corner of the couch.

"How do you do, sir. I'm Roger Ailes. I'm the executive producer." He looked up weakly, shook my hand, and softly said, "Jack Benny." He went on, "Tell me about your show." But he was talking in a monotone—very quietly—and I thought, "Oh my God, he's going to pass away right on the air today." I explained the show and where his segment would come. He asked, "Do you have a dollar bill?" I said yes. He said, "I'm going to do this thing with Mike using this dollar bill, where I end up getting the dollar." I said fine. We worked it all out, but I was terrified. I thought, "Maybe I shouldn't present him, because it will be so disillusioning to the American people."

We went down to the studio just before airtime. He was to be on first. We rehearsed his theme song, "Love in Bloom," with the band, and I showed him where he would enter. All this time he was shuffling along, with the weary steps of an old man.

Moments later, it was airtime. Mike Douglas said, "We've got a great thrill for you today. Ladies and gentlemen, our special guest, the great Jack Benny."

I held my breath. The band hit "Love in Bloom." Benny inhaled and energy seemed to enter his body. He looked sideways into the full-length backstage mirror and straightened up. I swear he grew an entire foot. He looked twenty-five years younger. He looked at me, smiled, and winked, and as the doors opened for his entrance, he broke into his famous arm-swinging stride and walked on stage. The real Jack Benny had suddenly appeared right before our eyes. On the show, he was the delightful, brilliant Jack Benny that we knew—age thirty-nine, as he always said—and that we all remember.

Benny's use of energy was a great lesson for me. He had been saving it for the performance, and he knew exactly when to turn it on. And I remember thinking something then that I still teach today. Know when you have to do a good job. Know when you're on. And anytime you perform, if your energy rises to the occasion, you'll carry the day.

LIFE FORCE

Since then, I have learned that you must use your own natural life force—the energy that we all have when we are interested in something and are just "being ourselves." That will make up for a variety of deficiencies in style and technique. I've seen many speakers who have good technique. They are gifted with a great voice, and they do everything that traditional approaches teach them to do, and yet the audience walks away bored or indifferent. I've also seen speakers without great voices and great techniques, but they are interesting, comfortable, and committed to what they're saying. The audience walks away enriched and happy because the experience was worthwhile. Strive to be that second kind of speaker—whether you're testifying in a courtroom or giving a tour of your city to out-of-town visitors. If the audience knows you care about what you're doing, you can forget about most speaking "techniques." Using your natural energy, or life force, when you communicate sends a strong, clear message to your audience that you are committed to what you're saying. Because you believe it, your listeners are much more likely to believe it, too.

RX FOR ENERGY CRISES

People often ask me, "How do you do this? How do you get your energy up?" I can't answer for everyone but I can answer for myself. The way I do it is simple. I've often been asked to go into an interview with a reporter when I'm exhausted. I usually sit quietly and collect my thoughts. I breathe deeply. Prior to going in, I think about the goals of the interview and I think about what the reporter wants to get out of the interview. I try to give the reporter as much as I can without doing anything damaging to myself. Then when I actually enter the room, I walk with confidence. Sometimes I will even walk around in the hall for a few minutes before I go in just to get my heart pumping. When I enter the room, I focus on the new person I'm meeting and find things to like about him. I concentrate very hard on that person: I ask a few questions about him and his background, why he's interviewing me, and what the article is about. All this time, the focus is off of me. Once I come through that doorway, I no longer think about myself. The reporter is either going to like me or not going to like me. He is either going to attack or not going to attack. There's not much I can do to change that. The only thing I can do is read the person, show that I'm not threatened by the situation, try to be as candid as possible, and try to help the reporter achieve his goals.

The same principles can be applied when you walk on stage to address an audience. Just focus on something other than yourself; walk around and be physically energetic. I've known people who go to the rest room prior to a speech and just vocalize, opening up their throats and loudly saying, "Ah, ah, ah." I've known people who do push-ups before a speech. Choose whatever works to get you physically engaged—not to the extent that you're breathless or hyperventilating, but just to the point where you feel a healthy glow before you walk in and deliver.

IN THE LION'S CAGE

As soon as you get into the room with a reporter or in front of an audience, move your eyes comfortably and in a random pattern, look directly at whoever is in the room, and smile. This demonstrates that you have no fear of the situation. Some people have the feeling that going before an audience is like going into a lion's cage. To me that's a negative thought. But even if I were to think that, I'd keep my eye on the lion. I sure wouldn't look at my feet, and I sure wouldn't look at the ceiling if I got into the lion's cage. So if it's more helpful for you to see it that way, fine. I don't see audiences as threatening, but if you do, just look at the lion!

I learned this lesson of energy and commitment very early in my career and in a particularly forceful way. I was an assistant director of a television program. One of the producers I worked for was very creative and could be charming, but he often displayed a brutal, sadistic personality. Frequently, he'd pick out a staff member and browbeat him or her all day long. It was very embarrassing to witness and humiliating to endure. Nobody liked it. But everybody put up with it because we were all afraid of him.

One day it was my turn to be in the barrel, as we called it. He started picking on me first thing and kept it up all morning. By two o'clock in the afternoon, I'd had it. I went right up to him, looked him in the eyes, and said, "That's it. Don't do that to me anymore." Well, he had to do it just one more time. That was unacceptable to me, so I took a swing at him. It turned into a regular brawl. We broke up some office equipment, and finally two guys dragged me into the men's room to end the fiasco.

I figured I'd just ruined my career. But actually it had quite the opposite effect. Two years later, that producer left the program and I was considered for his job, along with several others who were older and more experienced than me. One day, the company president called me to a meeting and told me he wanted to put me in charge of the whole operation. "We've got three reasons for picking you over the others," he said. "First, you can make other people believe that you can do what you say you'll do. We're going to gamble on you, Ailes, because we believe that you believe you can do it. That's valuable to us. The second reason is that you've demonstrated that you have creative ideas and are not afraid to try new ones. Third, two years ago you proved that you're nobody's boy. You're the only one who ever fought back. You showed guts and although your method was immature, we want someone who can make independent decisions."

I was not quite twenty-six years old and became a national television producer. When I took over the program, it was seen in about 32 cities. When I left the program three years later, we had built it to the phenomenal level of 180 cities.

COMMITMENT

Now I don't recommend you get into the fistfights in the office to win promotions. But you can see how much importance people place on commitment and on putting some energy behind your belief in that commitment.

Most people think that their energy level is much higher than it is. Eighty percent of our clients are surprised when they first see themselves on tape. They usually say things like "I thought I was more forceful," "I didn't know I was so boring," "I never move my face or hands," "I'm talking in a monotone." Most people think they're coming on too strong in a speech, when usually it's just the opposite. Whether you think your energy level is too high, too low, or just right, ask some of your friends what they think. You may be surprised at what you learn. Actually, you should always bring your energy up a little bit in front of an audience. Ninety-nine percent of us have natural inhibitions which will keep us from going too far. If you happen to be in the other one percent, your wife, husband, or friend can point it out, and it's easy to back off just a bit.

In our next chapter, we'll talk about a problem we all have at one time or another: taking things too seriously!

11
LIGHTEN UP, YOU'RE WEARING EVERYBODY OUT

I was once in a meeting with one of the most powerful chairmen in the entertainment industry—a much feared tyrant. Together with his top staff, we were discussing a television program I was producing for his corporation. The chairman was a temperamental man, and he proceeded to throw a fit over some minor scheduling problems. He yelled at everyone around the table. Like an irate prosecutor, he singled out and grilled each person, seeming to revel in his ability to intimidate. The tension was mounting. When he got to me, he shouted, "And you, Ailes, what are YOU doing?"

I said, "Do you mean now, this evening, or for the rest of my life?" There was a shocked moment of silence. The others in the room were wide-eyed, aghast. The chairman threw back his head and roared with laughter. Permission granted, the others laughed, too.

Humor broke the tension of a very uncomfortable scene. God knows we could use a few more laughs in this world. There's nothing more tedious than a person who takes himself too seriously.

THE BOTTOM LINE

If I had to summarize in two words the advice I give to many of my clients, it is "Lighten up!" For seven out of ten people who lose their jobs, the reason isn't lack of skill. According to studies by executive recruiters, it's personality conflicts. The flip side to that is reflected in this quote from the management newsletter *Bottom Line—Personal:* "As an executive reaches middle management and beyond, the primary criteria for advancement are communication and motivation skills, rather than basic job performance. Relations with superiors and peers are also critical. Bottom line: Top management promotes people it likes." What is guaranteed to make people not like you? Taking yourself too seriously.

You can always spot people who take themselves too seriously. Usually they are either brooding or talking a great deal about themselves. A positive ego can be the greatest ally in a communications situation, but negative ego can be the biggest detriment to your life. Whenever I see someone who talks a great deal about himself, I'm reminded of the old story about the actor who testified in court. The prosecuting attorney says to the actor who's on the stand, "Sir, who is the greatest actor of all time?" The actor says, "Me." The attorney says, "Isn't that a bit egotistical?" The actor says, "Perhaps, but I'm under oath."

YOUR RESPONSIBILITY

Those people fired because of personality clashes or "office politics" probably would still have their jobs if they had only eased up and gotten their egos out of the way, so that people looked forward to seeing them and working with them. The hard premise for many people to swallow is that easing up is *your* responsibility. If you truly hate your job or the people you work with, go somewhere else. But as long as you've decided to stay where you are, it's your responsibility to be enthusiastic, positive, and friendly.

Take a good hard look at your ego. Does it get in the way of your communications? Do you say ''I'' too often? Are you usually focused on your own problems? Are those problems out of proportion to reality? Do you complain frequently? Do you take every opportunity to tell others how tough you have it? When people tell you about a new idea, do you find a negative point to puncture their balloon? Do you believe fate has cheated you? Do you still blame your parents for some real or imagined slight to you?

EGO QUESTIONS

You may see all of these questions as simply negative. Well, they are. But they are more than that because they are all about you. They're ego questions. If you answered yes to even one of the questions, you need to lighten up. You're wearing out your friends, family, and coworkers. Lightening up implies humor and not taking everything too seriously. But it's part of your overall attitude. Do you bring other people up or down? This may be the most important question facing you in your career and your life.

A few years ago, an executive (let's call him Fred) was sent to me for communications training with this ultimatum from the exasperated chairman of his company: ''I'm on the brink of canning Fred, even though he's suffering from the delusion that he should have been promoted to president of his division. He does know more about that division than anybody in the company. He's brilliant at business planning and good at finding waste. But he never smiles and he's indecisive. He depresses the hell out of everyone with his hangdog look. When Fred comes down the hall, people dart into closets, run behind watercoolers, and dive under their desks to avoid getting infected with his gloom. He gets so preoccupied with the dark side of things that it stifles his decision-making abilities.

"Ailes, if this guy doesn't ease up, I'm gonna throw him off a cliff—before he makes me and everyone else want to jump."

HEIR APPARENT

When Fred came to my studio for the first time, he didn't have to say a word—it was all written on his face. He looked stricken, as if he'd just arrived at a funeral. When he spoke, his voice was monotonous, lifeless. He told me he was disappointed and hurt because he didn't get the promotion. After twenty years with the company, he had risen to executive vice president on the basis of several measurable accomplishments. When the president of the division retired, Fred saw himself as the heir apparent. But the chairman hired an outsider as president and told me that Fred was passed over because he lacked certain leadership skills. Fred's negative attitude caused him to always expect the worst. Because Fred always feared the worst, he delayed most decisions and sometimes became paralyzed.

DEAD UNCERTAIN

Talking with Fred for just a few minutes confirmed for me the chairman's assessment: Fred didn't have a clue why he had missed being promoted. To make it clear to Fred that his negative attitude and his indecisiveness were linked, my associate, Jon Kraushar, presented Fred with this role-playing situation: "The entire executive staff of your company has been at a retreat at The Greenbrier in West Virginia. On the return trip home, the plane they all took crashes, and everyone is killed. You didn't go on the trip because of a family emergency. So now you are the only surviving member of your company's top management team. I'm your second-in-command. You've just called me into your office to tell me what I'm supposed to do now. You alone are in charge of the company. What do you say?"

Fred's eyes widened. He looked frozen, like a rabbit in the headlights. He said, "What do you think?"

Jon replied, "You're in charge. What do you want me to do?"

Fred stared vacantly for a full fifteen seconds. Then he said, "Do you think we should call the families?" We purposely tossed the question back to Fred, who fumbled with it. The same thing happened when we asked questions like "How do you want to handle the announcement to company employees?" and "What about the news media?"

It was just chaos and we had it all on videotape. Fred was in shock. It was a brutal exercise, but it was absolutely necessary to show him that he wasn't ready to command the division.

Once he watched himself on videotape, he got the message. We discussed his need for some additional psychological counseling (he had been seeing an analyst). Our immediate goal was to save his job and make him perform better in the workplace. He thought he was very good at his job. However, his self-esteem was very low. He seemed to have no enthusiasm for anything—no energy or life force emanating from him. We first reviewed all of the good things he had done at work and the contributions he'd made to the company.

PART OF YOUR JOB

I went to the blackboard and wrote JOB DESCRIPTION. I said, "Let's define your job. Let's make sure you're doing all of it. You tell me you're great at your job and you should have been promoted. What are your duties, and what grades would give yourself on them?"

He went down the list, including financial management, strategic planning, and marketing. He gave himself high grades in each. When he finished, I said, "There are a couple of categories missing." I wrote down decisiveness and attitude. On decisiveness we gave him a very low grade and reminded him of the videotape when he was in charge of the whole company. On attitude, I said, "Part of your job is to be enthusiastic and upbeat, and you're failing. You're supposed to lead a team and inspire them. But you're getting an F there. You tell me you're not depressed, just serious. Well, perception is reality and everybody else thinks you're depressed. Even if you're not depressed, you're too damned serious. It's fine to be serious about your job or your life, but it appears as if you take everything and yourself way too seriously. That's why you didn't get that promotion. Not because your job skills are lacking, but because your attitude stinks."

I concluded, "Fred, I've got to tell you the truth. You depress me." He laughed. I persevered. "Fred, that's how your bosses view you. That's why people don't want to see you coming down the hall. Does your boss avoid meetings with you or cut them short?" Fred admitted that he did. Thinking about it, he turned pale, but it was sinking in. After meeting with us six more times over the next few months, he was able to accept that his attitude was part of his overall job description and that he had to lighten up. With some additional counseling Fred made a dramatic improvement at work and has assumed increased responsibilities.

To lighten up doesn't mean you become a comedian. But if you can appreciate humor and occasionally see the light side in stressful situations, you'll be the kind of person others enjoy being around.

A SENSE OF HUMOR

Almost everybody who comes to me for training would like to become more humorous. The general rule is, if you're not a humorous person in life, the chances of your becoming funny once a month for fifteen minutes during a speech are probably not too good. But if you're a relatively comfortable person off stage, you'll have a better chance of succeeding with humor when you get up to the lectern. That's because when you relax, your audience relaxes, and this allows them to be receptive to the humor you offer. The goal, you'll recall, is to be as comfortable a communicator on stage as you are when you're entertaining someone in your living room.

Occasionally someone comes to me and says, "I'd like to

learn to be funnier." I begin by asking a series of questions. Why don't you try to answer each of them?

YOUR HUMOR QUOTIENT

Who's your favorite comedian? Who or what do you think is funny? When was the last time you laughed out loud? When was the last time you chuckled? Have you ever made anyone laugh? When? And why was the situation funny? Do you know any jokes? Do you remember any time in your life when you laughed uncontrollably? Would your friends describe you as amusing in casual conversation? Who's your funniest friend? Picture a favorite comedy scene from a film. Describe it and tell me why it's funny.

If you had trouble answering any of these questions (as many of my clients do), you may have a higher interest in being humorous than in humor itself. If you don't (or can't) observe, understand, and enjoy humor, you won't be able to *use* it. I've had guys come in to me who looked like killers, acted like thugs, and wanted to tell jokes. These are not people who are going to get big laughs. They intimidate people.

OUTSIDE THE DOTS

You can begin to get a grasp on humor by reading "outside the dots," that is, outside of the normal reading you do for business purposes. Let's say someone's an engineer and he wants to be a good after-dinner speaker. It's unlikely that he'll glean a lot of laughs from reading *Principles of Thermodynamics* or *Elements of Plastic Extrusion Blow Molding.*

At a minimum, he could try scanning *Reader's Digest* for a humorous anecdote he might use. Most humor from joke-books or anthologies cannot be used verbatim. But if the idea is funny, you can rework the language to suit your style and the occasion.

Here's an example of a story adaptable to remarks before any professional group. R. T. McNamar, of the Treasury Department, told the California Association of Realtors this story about competition:

> Before I tell you about the good news I thought I might set the stage with a story that happened back in Prohibition days. It seems that 25 of San Francisco's top bootleggers were rounded up in a surprise raid. As they were being arraigned, the judge asked the usual question about occupation. The first 24, it seems, were all engaged in the same professional activity. Each claimed he was a realtor.
>
> "And what are you?" the judge asked the last prisoner.
>
> "Your honor, I'm a bootlegger," he said.
>
> Surprised, the judge laughed and asked, "How's business?"
>
> "It would be a lot better," he answered, "if there were not so many realtors around."[13]

It's tough to teach humor to a person who can't laugh at himself. How are you on that score? When was the last time other people laughed at you and you were able to laugh along? Think of something really foolish that you did. Would you be comfortable telling others about it and laughing along with them? Although you take your job seriously, can you see the funny side of it?

Economist Richard W. Rahn of the Chamber of Commerce of the United States told the Tax Foundation's thirty-second national conference this story as a lead-in to a discussion of supply-side economics:

> It's a pleasure to be here on the first day of real winter in New York. New York hasn't really changed, though, I've noticed. I got out of a cab this morning and a typical New York bum walked up to me and said, "May I have five dollars for a cup of coffee?" I had lived here for a couple of years while going to school and teaching here. It seemed to me the prices used to be lower, and I said, "Isn't five dollars an awful lot for coffee?" And the fellow said, "Well, you know, the money supply's been growing over 14 percent. That's M1B." I said, "Really?" and he said, "Yes, and the wage rates have been up an average level of about 11 percent, and it's been very difficult for us out here on the street." I said to this fellow, "Well, if you know all of

this, why don't you become an economist?" With that he reared back, stiffened up, looked me square in the eye and said, "Sir, I still have *some* pride left."[14]

The intensity some people bring to their jobs and, more importantly, to themselves can stifle humor. They cannot understand why everybody around them doesn't take them and their job as seriously as they do. The reality is, nobody cares as much as you do. Others may pretend they do. They may nod knowingly and look intent and compliment you, but running around behind their eyeballs is the feeling that "this guy is wearing me out. He is so intense about what he is doing. And he thinks it's so important that if he stops, the world stops."

THE SHOWMAN

Let me step outside the corporate world for a moment to tell you about a man who was a true professional, largely because he personified much of what I have just discussed. Whether you can identify with him or not, you can appreciate his lighthearted approach to his public life, combined with his enormous talent. I'm referring to Liberace.

Liberace was known to his friends as Lee. When he was a small boy growing up in Wisconsin, he had to play piano in beer halls to make money. His father was a very stern, somewhat humorless classical musician who insisted that Lee become a classical pianist. Lee reluctantly complied with his father's wishes. Finally, he was booked to play a classical concert and his father attended. Liberace performed at his best that night with an unusual flair. But when the concert ended and he turned toward his father's seat, hoping to see him beaming with pride, he saw that the seat was empty. His father had walked out of the concert. When Liberace arrived home, his father berated him for acting like a clown while performing great musical works. Liberace later said that his father's rejection that night was the greatest disappointment of his life. However, he went on to turn tragedy into triumph.

He later became known as the greatest showman since Al Jolson. Without a sense of humor he never could have turned his tears into laughter. He was pure show business through and through. He knew what worked for him; he didn't alter that. He never disappointed an audience, he did his homework, and he was able to take a joke on himself.

As a television producer, I worked with him several times, and he was a total professional. In the summer of 1981, I was in Las Vegas producing some special programs in the Fantasy Suite at Caesars Palace. One was to be an intimate, late night entertainment program and Liberace was scheduled as the primary guest. He was appearing at the hotel and had two shows to do in the main room. He agreed to make a brief appearance on our program and do one number on the piano. Unfortunately, everything that could go wrong did go wrong that day, and we were running over three hours behind schedule. It was almost two in the morning and we were still unable to tape. Liberace was exhausted from having appeared in two 70-minute shows already. When he arrived at our suite for taping, he quickly realized we were in trouble. Instead of leaving, he sat down at the piano and asked for requests from the crew to keep everybody in a good mood until we could get our technical problems solved. I remember seeing him there, exhausted, perspiring, but having a great time playing "Beer Barrel Polka" for the stagehands.

There have probably been more jokes about Liberace than about anybody in show business. He kidded about himself. And he became one of the most loved figures in the business. I don't think there was a single producer, performer, or writer anywhere who knew Liberace and didn't like him. He was a classic example of a man who never let you see the dark side. He was always smiling and he always had time for a kind word. When he was with people, Lee knew that *he* was what he had to sell. He was the message. And he never showed anything that interfered with the message. Here was a man who was a little different. Liberace was an extreme, of course, in dress and style.

But part of his legacy to us was to emphasize the importance of not taking yourself too seriously.

TO BE MORE HUMOROUS

I often recommend an exercise to people who want to be more humorous: Watch the opening monologue of "The Tonight Show." Tell me what makes you laugh about it, if anything. Watch Jay Leno and tell me why you think he's funny, or why he's not funny. Go to a theater and see the best comedy films today. Then, explain a scene from the movie that made you laugh. Elaborate on why that scene worked. Also, be prepared to talk about three people in your life who you think are funny or who make you laugh.

BEGIN WITH RESEARCH

The ability to do humor depends on the six Rs: research, relevance, rhythm, rehearsal, relaxation, and risk.

I believe strongly that you have to do research to find a story that you like. Research is the first of six Rs regarding good humor and storytelling.

A lot of people read stories and then think, "Gee, this must be funny because it's in a book or it's in a newspaper." They use it and it doesn't work. Often they don't believe in it themselves. I would never tell a story I didn't personally think was funny. A lot of research has to go into it. As you do casual reading, look for humorous ideas. There are many stories that, by changing the ending, altering the punch line, or getting rid of antiquated or inappropriate language within the story, can be turned into a pretty good modern-day story. Most people don't look at it that way. They take it at face value and say, "That's not funny," and therefore they don't use it. I've seen my friend, humorist Mort Sahl, read an afternoon newspaper and create several new laughs for that evening's performance. Very few of us are as good as Mort at creating humor, but it does point out that humor is right under our noses.

RELEVANCE

Of course, the critical element is to make the story relevant to what you're saying. Relevance is the second R. Relevance lets you get into and out of a joke. A joke rarely stands alone. It has to relate to the material that you're talking to the audience about.

When I give a speech about political polling, I like to tell the story of the fellow who moves to a new town. He goes down to the courthouse to try to make some new friends. He sees an old fellow sitting on the curb with a dog beside him. The new man in town walks over and asks, "Does your dog bite?" The old guy looks up at him and says, "Nope." So the fellow reaches down to pet the dog, and the dog nearly rips his arm off. He jumps back quickly and says, "I thought you said your dog doesn't bite." The old guy looks up and says, "Ain't my dog."

Well, that fellow just didn't ask the right question. That story gets me into the importance of asking the right questions when doing polls.

RHYTHM

The next important point about storytelling in front of an audience is to get the rhythm of the joke. Rhythm is the third R. Many people expand jokes rather than contract them. They think that by adding more words and giving more detail, it will make the story funnier. Usually it makes it less funny. The quickest, cleanest way to get to the punch line is usually the best. The only exception might be a shaggy-dog story, designed to go on and on absurdly. But you have to be a master storyteller to pull that off. Stories have a natural beginning (setup), middle (information/conflict), and end (payoff/punch line). If you disturb the rhythm, you can kill the laugh.

REHEARSAL

Before I'd get up at a dinner party to tell a joke for the first time, I'd tell it to my family. Or I'd tell it to a friend. Rehearsal is the next R. You've got to rehearse the story or joke out loud, preferably to others who'll react to it spontaneously. I'd work on it in a few places so that I had the rhythm of it down, hitting the right word at the right time, taking the pause at the right time, delivering the punch line at the right time, not physically moving on the punch line. Just do a little practice before you tell it in public. Even highly paid professional comedians like Steve Martin, Robin Williams, Rodney Dangerfield, and Eddie Murphy drop into small comedy clubs and work for nothing just to try out new material.

RELAXATION

After research, relevance, rhythm, and rehearsal comes relaxation. It's not the end of the world if your joke doesn't work. Sometimes it won't. Interestingly enough, the audience will always give you a higher grade for effort than for not trying, as long as you don't embarrass them. The only way you can keep from embarrassing them is to avoid being embarrassed yourself. Be comfortable. Stay relaxed. If you give the story a try and it doesn't quite work, just keep moving ahead with your remarks or kid yourself for bombing. The world won't end. If you can, have your performance audio- or videotaped. Study the tape. Listen to your voice. Why did the story work or not work? Keep trying. It's worth it. There's no greater feeling than hearing an audience laugh at something you say. I know many serious actors who would give up their careers to make audiences laugh.

RISK

Finally, there is a reasonable risk in humor, and many people simply don't want to take that risk. They'll settle for the general embarrassment of not being a good speaker, rather than the highly specific embarrassment of a joke that doesn't work. The most important thing to do is not set up any joke or story as the funniest thing in the world. Just segue into it and tell it. Either it works or it doesn't. Life goes on. If you've done the Rs, you can at least count on a few smiles. Just stay comfortable and keep moving.

Many people have become good storytellers with this system, so I know it works!

12
OKAY, AILES, FIX ME: THE AILES METHOD/ COURSE

Two types of clients come to us for communications coaching. Some clients want to improve at everything. They see themselves on a fast track. They want to move up quickly, and they recognize that communications is going to help them. Those in the second group are sent by someone else, usually from their company. These clients are dragged in kicking and screaming, and they don't want anybody to mess with them.

The first type of client—the "can do" type—usually is already pretty good at speaking and wants to get better. The second type is the "can't do" type. My favorite of the second type was an entrepreneur sent to me by a financial consultant. He came in, sat down in front of my desk, folded his arms, crossed his legs, slouched down in the chair, scowled, and said, "Okay, Ailes, fix me."

I knew immediately that here was trouble. This was a very successful entrepreneur who had built a multimillion-dollar company on his own. But now he was going to expand, and he needed to go to Wall Street to raise more money. This meant he would be standing up in front of investment bankers, making a pitch, asking for help. Up to this point, he'd been spectacularly unsuccessful at this. So he was sent to me, and he resented it.

I asked, "What are you so scared of?"

"Nothing. I didn't get where I am by being scared. I'm a multimillionaire and I worked my way up from nothing. Now I've got to go to Wall Street and talk to those silver-spoon jerks about giving me some money."

"Well, apparently you're failing at that."

He blanched but said nothing.

"Let's go into the studio and see what's going on." I rolled the camera and said, "Just stand up there and start making the same request for money that you do on Wall Street. Tell me about your business and why I should invest."

THE FIRST THIRTY SECONDS

I let him talk for about thirty seconds, and then I stopped him and asked, "What are you afraid of?"

"Nothing."

"Why are you angry?"

"I'm not angry."

"So far I've seen five visible signs of fear and hostility and you're only thirty seconds into your pitch." I stopped the tape and played it back.

The tape showed him using inflammatory words, with his hands in front of his face and his eyes up to the ceiling. He built himself up too much. He had a wary look on his face and folded his arms as if to protect himself. He made just about every conceivable mistake.

I told him, "I think what's happening here is that you're a self-made man—you didn't get a business degree—and you feel far more successful than the people from whom you have to raise money. And you resent them because you think Wall Street people inherited their money and never had to scramble—they went to preppy schools in the East which you couldn't afford. So, as you face them, you're dumping all this hostility and anger out on them. And frankly, pal, if I were one of them, I wouldn't give you a nickel."

Again I played the tape back and froze it at certain points for him, to explain what I meant. He just slumped down in his chair and said, "Oh my God, I had no idea."

AN ALTERNATIVE APPROACH

We worked for a while. But I still couldn't get him to ease up enough. Finally, we took a break and I asked him if he had any children. He said he did. So I told him, "Pretend that your kids have asked you to come over and talk to their class about what you do for a living." We rolled the tape again and he just extemporized about his company, its product, its history, his plans to expand the business and make it even more profitable. He was terrific and very likable. A whole different side of his personality had emerged. After we watched the replay together I said, "Now, if you talked to me this way, I'd be more likely to consider your proposal."

Apparently Wall Street agreed, because a couple of months later, he reached his financial goal.

"IMAGE"

In my business, we refer to ourselves as communications consultants. Some people, though, like to call us image makers. The truth is, no one can manufacture an image for anyone. If you want to improve or enhance yourself in some way, the only thing a consultant can do for you is to advise and guide you. We can point out assets and liabilities in your style, and we then offer substitutions and suggestions to aid you. You have to want to improve and work at it. Most importantly, whatever changes you make have to conform to who you really *are*—at your best. All the grooming suggestions, all the speech coaching, all the knowledge about lighting, staging, and media training—everything popularly associated with "image making"—won't work if the improvements don't fit comfortably with who you essentially are.

CHECKLIST

One of the tools we use to diagnose "you at your best" is a simple checklist of items. It includes physical appearance, energy, rate, pitch, tone, phrasing, gestures, eye contact, and holding an audience's interest. Let's say we videotaped you in a session in my New York studio. When we replay the tape, we hand you the list and say, "Imagine you don't know this person on the screen, and just fill in your impressions next to the items on the list. I've called you in now to give me your advice. What do you think of this person you're watching? What do you think of this person's voice, his use of language, his descriptive abilities, the way he moves, the way he makes you feel?"

What's interesting here is that most people score themselves either too high or too low. Very few people actually hit it right. That tells us something about their self-image, which gives us a place to start. Some people, so as not to show great vulnerability, will say, "You know, I think it's pretty good." They'll puff it up. Other people will say, "Boy, that's awful." You can see the blood drain from their faces.

What we've found about the people who describe themselves pretty accurately is that they generally are fairly secure people. They can usually take criticism pretty well and often display a certain amount of humor. It's very important for us to determine early on in the course how much positive and negative feedback we can safely give. If people have low self-esteem and think they're terrible at everything, they need to get some positive feedback before they can work on problems. There are always some good things about what they do, and we have to be able to point out those qualities. But in order to help them, I have to give them an honest assessment. It's always good to remind ourselves of our good points, because these assets are a foundation we can build on to become even better. Make a list of what you consider to be your strengths as a communicator.

Then ask a friend, a coworker, or others who know you well to tell you what they consider to be your strengths, especially as they relate to the way you communicate. Review the lists and consider whether some of the qualities are really *over*-strengths. For example, someone described as "persistent" might actually overdo it and become a pest. Or "eloquent" might be a polite term for someone who talks too much.

CANDOR

My job is to identify the strengths and weaknesses of my clients—and to draw the line between the two with a mixture of honesty and diplomacy. Many people who contact me are in a difficult position, such as the vice president of public relations who recognizes that his CEO needs some speech coaching. It's difficult for someone on the inside to critique his boss with complete candor and objectivity. In some cases, bluntness is needed. That's why it's helpful to bring in an outside consultant who can get in the same room with him and tell him like it is.

We usually work one-on-one so that we can be more candid. I believe in as much candor as the client can take, and many successful people want just that. However, we take care not to put anyone in an embarrassing situation.

I had an executive ask me recently what his real problem was. I said, "You're boring."

He was startled, but then started to laugh. "You know," he said, "I always thought that, but nobody ever said it."

I wouldn't say that to every client because some couldn't handle it. My job is to be sensitive to the needs of the client. But this guy was boring. Deep down he knew it and wanted to know how to be less boring. So we worked on it.

I asked him what he read, what he listened to, what he was involved in outside of his work. It turned out that years ago he had been a musician. In college he was in theater. When he began to open up, he was pretty interesting.

I videotaped him as we talked, and once he got into some

subjects that interested him, he came alive. Later, he could see that on tape.

Once people see themselves doing well, it's much easier for them to "play the tape back" mentally and perform better.

The hardest thing for me is to get clients *not* to change when the situation changes. Sometimes, before I can convince them to just act naturally, I try to capture them on videotape in an unselfconscious moment. Once we see the model behavior, that's usually the way I want them to come across in every communications situation. Behavior shouldn't change when the situation changes. They may need to slow down or talk a little louder. But basically they should be the same whether I put them on tape, go out to dinner with them, or put them in front of an audience.

MIRROR

In essence, we hold a mirror up to people. We say, "Take a look. Here's what other people see. What do *you* think?" Then we guide the impressions, because if the client says, "Gee, I really look terrible and, oh, I sound awful," and so on, we're there to put things into perspective. I even had to tell one client, "Ease up on yourself. You're successful." He was so tightly wrapped, so driven, that he drove other people up the wall. He was unrelenting to others and to himself.

THE HUNDRED-YEAR VIEW

When I work with someone like this, I encourage him to take what I call the hundred-year view: In a hundred years, will the thing that's giving you ulcers *really* be one of the highlights in the recorded history of the human species? Or would it be a better idea to take a little of the pressure off yourself and others?

When I was a young TV producer, I was so driven that one of the station executives said to me, "Ailes, I believe if I asked you to single-handedly move this building around the block over the weekend, you'd find a way." Some of this bulldoggedness was admirable. But for a while there, it threatened to burn me out. One day, a senior producer who was fond of me took me aside and gently suggested that I should take my work seriously, but not myself so seriously. Since then, I have often found myself having a good laugh when work pressures are at their height. "In a hundred years," I say to myself, "Who'll care?" (Think about that the next time you get very full of yourself.)

THE TRANSFORMATION

Some people say, "Don't change me. I know who I am, and I don't want to be changed." With these people I first record them in conversation before they're aware they're being taped, and they are quite good . . . warm, interesting, and comfortable.

Then I say, "Would you walk up to the lectern and give me a five-minute extemporaneous speech on your job?" Immediately they change into entirely different people. It's as though I turned my back and someone else took their place. They become very stiff and formal. And cold. They're often not aware that they've changed.

Afterward, we play back the two recordings and I show them the contrast in their two performances. This helps them over their fear of being changed, because they can see themselves changing and that our goal is to help them to stay themselves—in that warm, likable mode.

We record our clients in a series of formats—conversation, extemporaneous speaking, and reading a speech. By the end of the first hour, we have a pretty good idea of what we think is going on. We then try to elicit what the client would like to improve, because if we try to work on an area where he thinks he's terrific, we're not going to get very far.

The company sponsoring the client usually has a perspective on the problem, too. We combine our perception, the company's, and the individual's to find a common ground. Then we ask, "What would you like to improve?" From this, we can focus the training and develop it individually along these lines.

"I'M NOT AN ACTOR"

Another variation on "Don't change me" is the executive who tells me, "I'm not an actor. I don't want to learn to act. I'm *me*. I want to be me. I've been successful being me. I'm a successful person. I can't change now." They get all lathered up, and when I agree with them, they're nonplussed. "You mean I don't have to *act?*" they ask in these small, relieved voices.

I explain that I'm not going to teach them how to act. That would take years. Besides, acting isn't the skill required for effective communication of your *own* ideas. Acting is when someone asks you to be somebody *other* than who you really are. He or she hands you a script and asks you to play a part. On the other hand, performing is being *you at your best*. Most of us have seen actors appear as talk show guests. Some of them disappoint us because, when being *themselves*, they don't have the same aura, command, or even charm that they portray in their roles. On the other hand, those who *are* impressive personal communicators when *being themselves* have only used their acting training to be more comfortable in front of the camera or, perhaps, to move and gesture gracefully. The real meat of what they have to say comes from their off-screen or off-stage communication skills—especially their commitment.

There are many trained actors who also are effective personal communicators. Four who come to mind are Paul Newman, Liv Ullmann, Charlton Heston, and Katharine Hepburn. When they speak personally in an interview, they are performing, as opposed to acting. Again, performing is being *you at your best*.

We all perform at one time or another. In fact, every time you're asked to make a presentation, you're asked to be yourself at your best.

DON'T BE AFRAID TO PERFORM

Don't be frightened by the word "performing." Accept it. It's real. It's true. We all must do it and we all must do it well to be persuasive. It does not mean anything false. Remember, performing is simply being *you* at your best.

There's a natural momentum to life that distracts most of us from focusing on being better communicators. At the dinner table, we'll say, "Please pass the salt" and we get it. Many people assume they're communicating all right because, on a mundane level, they're getting what they want. But in the world of business, where time, information, and competition are factors, the communications skills required to get what you want are more demanding. You need to exert more energy than you do at the dinner table.

Times have changed in corporate America. At one time, the most qualified person got the job. Today, in a situation where three people with equal qualifications are interviewed for a job, the one with the best communications skills gets it. This becomes a bigger consideration every year.

The public image of a company is very important today. For recruiting, for advertising, for reaching the public, for being involved in the community, or for representing the company abroad—the person in charge has to be very good at presenting the company image to the public.

JOB INTERVIEWING

One of the most important communications situations you can be in is a job interview. Some of my senior executive clients find themselves out in the job market, either because they've been fired or because they've quit. They first go to an "outplacement consultant," where they get a great resume written and typed. They think that's going to get them a job.

A resume gets them in the door—maybe—but after that, the job interview is everything. Unfortunately, most senior executives haven't interviewed since they got out of college, and maybe not even then, because they were probably recruited. Suddenly they're sitting on the other side of the desk, and it can be a very traumatic, terrifying experience.

One of our clients for this type of training was a woman who was leaving a prestigious consulting firm. She was very good at her work, was highly paid, and had a formidable resume, but she was having trouble finding another job.

After listening to her for half an hour, I said, "We wouldn't hire you."

"Why?"

"Because you're looking for something in the neighborhood of $150,000 a year. I've listened to you talk about what you've done for clients for half an hour and you have not once addressed the bottom line. In other words, I can't precisely determine how I would get my $150,000 back if I hired you. Are you going to save it for me because of your work? Or are you going to bring in new business to compensate for it? Whenever I hire somebody in that range, I want to know how I'm going to make my money back plus. If you don't tell me how you did that for past employers or clients, you won't be hired."

We worked with her on communicating the tangible value of her skills and accomplishments, including their potential monetary worth to an employer. This type of training is usually done by us in three sessions. But after the second session, this woman was hired by a new company at a 25 percent increase in compensation.

CHECKLIST

If you ever find yourself in the job market (or know someone who is), you might find the following questionnaire and checklist helpful to review in preparing for a job interview. In fact, even when you're employed, it is helpful to be sure you can address these issues:

1. How is my physical appearance? Am I dressed and groomed appropriately for the job, the company, and the industry culture?

2. How self-assured do I seem? Can I put the interviewer (or others) at ease?

3. Can I communicate the following during the interview in a clear, brief, and interesting manner?

- How I represent a return on the employer's total investment in my pay and benefits if I'm hired (for example, I'll bring in x amount of business and I'll add measurable value to the company)
- Specific examples of my achievements at work, each delivered in no more than a one-minute "mini–case history" (focused on results, not activity)
- My knowledge of the industry (marketplace, products, personal contacts, inside and outside pressures)
- Knowledge of my potential employer's company (including its goals, challenges, history, and top management)

4. Can I demonstrate with concrete examples my:

- Maturity and readiness to take on responsibility
- Desire and enthusiasm to learn and grow on the job
- Positive attitudes toward management and coworkers
- Commitment and involvement: doing more than the basic job requires
- Understanding of the technical language and the practices of the industry

Here are some dos and don'ts for the interview (these also apply to communicating on the job).

DO

- Ask questions about relevant issues like job responsibilities, management practices, the assignments of coworkers, and performance reviews (how often, with whom, how done).
- "Bridge" or segue to a discussion of your skills. Relate your abilities to your potential boss's (or the company's) needs.
- Sit and walk upright, comfortably, and confidently. Look the interviewer in the eye. Smile.

• Listen actively. Nod and show interest with your eyes and face.

• Ask the interviewer to clarify anything you're unsure of.

• Be concise. Don't overexplain. If in doubt, ask, "Is that what you wanted to know?"

• Ask if you can provide additional background on yourself.

DON'T

• Slouch
• Fiddle with your hair, glasses, pen, or clothing
• Avert your eyes
• Mumble
• Criticize former employees, bosses, or coworkers
• Be too aggressive or arrogant
• Argue with your interviewer
• Apologize for any of your shortcomings

ONE THAT GOT AWAY

Although our female client found a new job quickly, not every story has been a success. Shortly after starting my own company, around 1971 or 1972, I gave someone's money back after the second session. I'd spent two hours working with him and played back the tape, and I swear to you he was worse!

In retrospect, I didn't establish the proper rapport with him in the beginning. I failed to do what I counsel others to do, and that is to make the other person comfortable. I clearly didn't make him comfortable. Because of that, he was completely unwilling to let go and try anything. Fortunately, I had enough positive reinforcement from other clients at the time to keep on going. Otherwise, I might have gotten out of the business because that was so depressing.

A key ingredient of success in our work is that our clients feel safe. They know our training is confidential, so they feel free to talk about themselves. They often tell me about traumatic experiences they've had in speaking situations.

EYE DART

One of my clients was a young female executive, a graduate of one of the top business schools in the country. She was very charming, very smart, very articulate. But her eyes shifted all over the room. She was nervous and it was coming out through her eyes. She couldn't make eye contact.

What we discovered was that this was a cultural thing for her. She's Eastern European and was taught that women don't hold eye contact with another person, whereas in America it's totally acceptable to look into the other person's eyes. We discussed the problem and had her watch herself on videotape to see how distracting it was.

CAN'T HEAR YOU

Occasionally, someone will come in and mumble, "I don't know why I'm here."

I'll say, "What? I didn't hear you."

This is an obvious problem. This person has to learn to project his voice clear across the table. But if his world is charts and forecasts and numbers, he may not have to do that at work. So with him, we work first on helping him to become aware of how to amplify his voice, then on increasing volume comfortably.

I mentioned earlier that at my company we "hold up a mirror" to the people we coach. Actually, it's a three-part process. As the Chinese say, there are three mirrors that form a person's reflection. The first mirror is how you see yourself. The second mirror is how others see you. The third mirror is how you really are. We move our clients to that third mirror by combining their descriptions of themselves, the feedback others have given them, and our observations into a frank discussion of who they really are.

A HOT DOG AT FIFTY-THREE

For example, I had one client—a $600,000-a-year man—whom I asked to describe himself. He told me that he had always been the bright young man of the company. He was fifty-three. I had to tell him that he was fifty-three but acted like twenty-three. We had a serious discussion, and he could also look on the tape and see how he came across as a hot dog. A hot dog at twenty-three is okay, but a hot dog at fifty-three just doesn't fit. (Could this be you?)

Like everyone else, I have my own personal way of working. Many of my perceptions come when I go off to my study alone and watch a videotape for a few minutes.

If I'm having trouble putting my finger on clients' problems, there's one technique I can always count on: getting in touch with how they make me feel. In essence, I become their audience.

WHAT'S GOING ON?

Sometimes, I'll look at a tape with the sound turned off and try to examine my feelings just watching how a person moves. Then I'll ask myself, "Is there anything going on here that makes me want to turn the sound up?" It's an emotional thing. And often I tell the client, "Look, I don't see any technical problems in what you're doing. I can only tell you what I feel."

Professor Albert Mehrabian of the University of California, Los Angeles, conducted an extensive research project in which he studied many different speakers and audiences to determine which factors most influenced listener impressions. His findings might surprise some people. Professor Mehrabian discovered that audiences' interpretations of messages are determined 55 percent by the speaker's nonverbal communication (facial expression, body language), 38 percent by the speaker's voice (quality, tone, pitch, volume, variation) and only 7 percent by the words themselves. This doesn't mean that words are unimportant. But audiences generally process words as indications that you can "speak the language" of your subject. Some of your words may be powerful or catchy enough to remember. But what audiences remember overall are two things. First, concepts—the idea clusters formed by the words. Second, your emotional expression as communicated through your eyes, face, voice, and body. The total package (composite) of these elements makes up the speaker, and the speaker becomes the message.

FEAR

The one overriding element which can distort your message is fear. It's the major block to clear, crisp communications. Many people think they must conquer fear once and for all. They spend their lives jousting with fear—but never win a clear victory.

Fear is a natural emotion in all humans, and we must learn to live with it. Keeping fear in perspective and converting it to positive energy is the secret. We'll discuss that in our next chapter.

13
EVEN HEROES GET SCARED

If you've ever had to get up and give a speech, did your stomach tighten, your palms sweat, and your throat dry up? If that's ever happened to you, then you should read this chapter, because otherwise it is going to happen again.

In a poll of human fears, twice as many people were more afraid of speaking in public than of dying. I believe that fear of failure and embarrassment are the biggest reasons people don't do certain things in life—including speaking in front of an audience.

ARE YOU READY?

Once on a television show, we had as a guest a Marine Corps general who had won a congressional Medal of Honor for his service in Vietnam. *Life* magazine had written about his courage.

I went backstage just before airtime and asked, "General, are you ready?" He said, "I'm not going on." I had planned twenty minutes of the program around him, so I said, "General, this is not a good time to tell me you're not going on. The show starts in five minutes." He choked out the words again: "I'm not going on." He looked ashen. He was clearly terrified by the prospect of appearing on a national television show. If he didn't go on, the show would be a disaster; I had to think quickly. I finally said, "General, let me put it this way. In just a few minutes you will be introduced, and either you're going to walk out there and talk or I'm going on in place of you and tell everybody you're chicken." There was a long pause. He was huge, and I thought he was going to pound me into the floor. But then he smiled. First he got a smile in his eyes, and then his face smiled, and it seemed to relax him. He seemed to gain energy from the challenge I'd thrown at him. He went on the show. He was a little shaky starting. His throat was tight and he gave one-word answers. But after the first couple of minutes, he was fine.

TEMPORARY PARALYSIS

The temporary paralysis that the general experienced was for years known as "stage fright." Dressed up in psychological lingo, today it's often referred to as "performance anxiety." Whatever you call it, you certainly know when you have it. The most common symptoms are increased heartbeat, a queasy feeling in the stomach, sweating, trembling, quick breathing as if gasping for air, dry mouth, and difficulty vocalizing. Due to stress, the vocal cords often tighten, choking off normal, relaxed speech and sometimes causing the voice to crack. Most of us don't get all of these symptoms at once, but even experienced speakers feel some of them some of the time.

Stage fright has been compared to what psychologists call the fight-or-flight syndrome. This is the decision humans make when confronted by a threat. They either run away from it or take it on. The prehistoric caveman spotted a wild boar in the jungle and he either hightailed it out of there or took up his cudgel. Our contemporary fight-or-flight situations usually imperil our egos more than our lives. When we are asked to face an audience, the atavistic instincts remain in us: Do we retreat or charge ahead?

That's the first decision anyone has to make when faced with stage fright. I pushed the general to that decision and he reverted to character. He decided to fight.

PERSPECTIVE

He put his fears into perspective. He contrasted his temporary anxiety with the longer-term confidence he felt about himself. I joshed him into seeing how absurd it was that a man with the courage to dodge bullets would dodge an interview. Once he smiled about the funny dissonance of these messages, he was able to relax a bit and return to who he was—a man of courage. Interestingly, courage isn't the absence of fear. It is action in the presence of fear. That's what it takes to overcome stage fright. The general was still afraid of going on television. But because he had enough inner strength, he decided to grapple with the fear instead of submitting to it.

You handle your fears in direct relationship to your inner strength. If you feel confident as a person, you can admit weakness, even fear and anxiousness, and not imperil your mission. Your self-image is strong.

SHORT-RANGE VERSUS LONG-RANGE

But overcoming self-image problems, at least on a temporary basis, is the real challenge. Performance anxiety results when you get nervous that all of your weaknesses over your whole life will become apparent in what is actually a short-range situation—for example, a particular speech, or even saying a prayer or making a toast at a holiday meal.

What many people tend to focus on is "I need to overcome all of my weaknesses and anxieties here and now. I need to be more handsome, more charming, more articulate, funnier, more intelligent."

But that's the impossible dream. So the anxious speaker stands backstage and says to himself, "When they introduce me, I need to be all these things which I'm not. I've spent my whole life trying to be those things and I didn't make it."

Instead, they need to ask themselves, "What is important right this minute? What do these people need or want to know right now? Why was I selected to speak on this subject? And how can I best communicate it?"

That puts the situation into perspective. It's like putting a cockroach under a magnifying glass. It looks like the star of one of those Japanese monster movies. Enlarged. The bug looks as though it could eat you. Get rid of the magnifying glass. It's just a cockroach. Step on it.

People with stage fright tend to put their whole self-worth and value against, say, 1 hour when they attend a meeting and give a speech. But there are about 720 hours in a month. Don't judge yourself just on the basis of 1 hour before an audience. Your place in history probably will not be determined by what you say in 1 specific hour.

It's a mental process to overcome stage fright. You have to say, "I have a right to be here. What I have to say is of value to this audience. I am an authority on this subject." Use whatever works to overcome your obsession with all your lifelong insecurities.

THE BEST RIGHT NOW

Because *you* are the message, you must view yourself in both a short-term and a long-term way. Long-term, it is valuable for you to try to improve yourself and your abilities constantly, thus striving to broadcast a clearer signal of a better you over a lifetime. But as with playing golf, when you're faced with a specific situation, you should play the best game of golf you've got right now. That means use everything you've got in your power at the moment and forge ahead. Missing a golf shot does not make you a hopeless, unathletic, lifelong jerk. Stumbling a little in a speech does not make you an inarticulate fool for life.

The process of putting fear into perspective will vary from person to person. The controller of a large financial services company suffered from stage fright so severe that he believed it would derail his career. My associate, Jon Kraushar, taped this man in our New York studio, first in conversation, then at the lectern doing a slide presentation which he had delivered, under duress, to his company's board of directors. Jon also observed the controller making brief remarks before a live audience. The amazing thing was that, in both cases, the man was a very good speaker! He had an excellent dry wit. He was knowledgeable and interesting. Because of his inner anxiety he didn't show as much commitment to his subject as he might have. However, contrary to his worst fears, he appeared to be comfortable. The live audience, in fact, gave him hearty applause when he finished.

THE MIND

Where then was this man's stage fright? In his mind. In conquering his fear, he found it helpful to watch himself on tape. He slowly realized that the perception he had of himself as a speaker was much less flattering than the reality.

THE WORST

When I feel anxious before I make a speech, I ask myself, "What is the absolute worst thing that can happen to me in this speech?" The answer is I can blank out. The audience could get up and leave—or worse, they could stay and derisively laugh at me. They could have secretly brought in bags of groceries to throw at me. Perhaps I'll humiliate myself in front of everyone else on the dais and never be able to give a speech again. That would be the end of my business. I'd be destroyed and never be able to get a job. Then I ask myself, "How likely is this to happen, even if I did blank out for a moment?" Of course, it's all nonsense. But by thinking that's the worst thing that could happen and knowing it won't, I'm able to realize that the situation is simply not that critical. I can laugh at myself and my inordinate amount of fear about speaking. Sure it's important to do well, but it's not life and death. Keep in mind one other thing as you move toward the lectern. You are an authority on what you are about to say. No one in the audience knows the subject better than you do. Therefore, you can draw on a certain amount of positive ego and approach the speaking situation with confidence.

TWO KINDS OF ANXIETY

There are two kinds of anxiety: exogenous anxiety, caused by frightening outside situations that may occur (like giving a speech), and endogenous anxiety, which is actually a disease caused by internal anxiety or panic. Very few people (probably less than 2 percent) actually suffer from endogenous anxiety. The rest have normal anxiety attacks at understandable times for logical reasons. If you recognize that this fear isn't something that's inherent in you, then it becomes a matter of controlling your externally induced fear.

ANTIDOTE TO FEAR

If you've read how-to books, you've been told that a normal amount of fear in a tense communication situation (like firing an employee or delivering a eulogy) is not only reasonable but good. Well, I don't disagree entirely with that. However, only a minimal amount of anxiety and fear is necessary if you are prepared. The single greatest antidote to fear is preparation. If you know exactly what you're going to do when you get in front of other people, you will do it and the fear will disappear immediately. The most important moment in communicating is that moment of beginning. There are two things every speaker should know besides what he's going to talk about: how to begin and how to end. Actually, it's nothing new. Vaudeville performers had their openings and their closings down cold. Every communicator must do the same. If you launch properly and with confidence, you will forget anxiety and your speech will go well.

Why doesn't every speaker do it if it's that simple? The reason is they don't plan *exactly* what they're going to say in the first thirty to sixty seconds. That is an absolute must. If you have to write it down, word for word, do it. But then transfer it into an outline form so that you're not staring at a piece of paper when you say, "I'm happy to be here." Do the same thing with your closing, and know that you can go to your closing at any one of several moments within a speech or talk. Even if you're on the telephone, speaking to a potential customer, you need to know how to grab his attention and how to sum up your main points. If you sense that you've been talking too long, cut it short and go to your ending paragraph. If you will work out the opening and closing of your remarks, you will never fail as a communicator—assuming, of course, that you have something to say in the middle. And more importantly, you will never be really afraid.

THE PILL

A large number of people come to me and say that when they first stand up to speak, they're frightened. One of my clients said, "I've tried everything and I'm still petrified." A week later he was having a physical, and he told his doctor about his stage fright and its accompanying symptoms, including heart palpitations and sweating. His doctor prescribed a drug called propranolol, used to treat patients suffering from hypertension, migraine headaches, and various heart ailments. Propranolol is classified as a "beta blocker" drug. It generally lowers hyperstimulation of the cardiovascular system.

My client pronounced propranolol his "magic potion." It at least relieved him of his anxiety symptoms. Eventually, with the skills learned in my training course, he was able to stop taking the drug.

I relate his experience in the interest of sharing information and not to recommend taking propranolol or any other drug (including alcohol) to calm fright symptoms.

According to medical authorities, propranolol is not a narcotic or a sedative. Therefore, it is said to be nonaddictive and won't make you sleepy. Some professional performers, including musicians and actors, use propranolol to combat stage fright.

If you wish to learn more about propranolol, you must consult with a doctor. The drug reportedly is dangerous for certain people, including those who suffer from diabetes, asthma, or hay fever. It may also cause side effects, such as light-headedness, nausea, and insomnia.

Despite my client's enthusiasm, propranolol is not a "magic potion." It may be a short-term tool. But the real "magic" to effective communication is found inside of you.

THE BIG RED ARROW

When some of us stand up in front of an audience, we have a tendency to feel that this big red arrow is pointing at us. In other words, we've lost all perspective. We don't see the audience. We don't focus on our topic. This huge arrow has a sign on it saying, "Ah, get him! Get him!" We think the whole world is looking at us and judging us. If we can psychologically turn the arrow around and aim it toward the audience, we can take the pressure off ourselves, because the longer we think the arrow's pointing at us, the more the pressure builds.

There are simple techniques to get over this. One is breath control. As the anxiety increases in a speech situation, your chest and throat muscles tighten and your breathing gets constricted. It's a vicious cycle. As you start gasping for breath, you get more frightened. When this happens, calm yourself by breathing deeply just before you move to the lectern. Inhale deeply through the nose, exhale through the mouth. Inhale again, not as deeply, exhale again. Then start speaking.

HEY BARNEY!

The fear of speaking in front of an audience must date back to early civilization, when the cavemen used to sit around the campfire at night and say, "Hey, what did you do today?" As long as they were in conversation, everyone was comfortable. But as soon as someone clanged his bone on his stone cup and said, "Barney, you get up and tell us what you did today," the rest of the people hushed up. There's Barney wearing his bearskin, standing before his peers cast in the light of a roaring fire. He's no longer part of the group. He's separated from the pack, and he has a different feeling. He feels anxious because he's now being judged by others. So, to the extent that we can make ourselves feel a part of the group, we can continue the relaxed, secure feeling and the confidence that we have in conversation. That goes to the heart of what we discussed earlier, that good speech is really nothing more than good conversation on your feet.

THE PERFECTION BLOCK

The one way to fail in a public speech situation is to try to be perfect. Perfection is the sure route to failure, because it complicates your life and creates so much more stress.

Many "how to speak" books suggest that you can make a speech perfectly and, with practice, can be so skilled that you will never make a mistake. But I say *it's okay if you make a mistake.* I tell our clients to put a speech into the category of human activity as opposed to computer activity or precision activity.

Of course, you should have your facts straight. You should not be sloppy. You cannot be unprepared. But you shouldn't believe you've failed if you didn't do everything *perfectly.* And unfortunately, many businesspeople are trained to be perfect and that's why they're not good public speakers.

OVERDRIVE

I see the perfection block very often among senior executives. They are driven people.

Drive played a major part in their success and, along with that, the desire to be perfect. The perfection syndrome is especially true of those who come from engineering, finance, or science, where precision is absolutely necessary for their success. So they apply the same standards to communications. The trouble is, their version of "perfection" when speaking translates to an overcontrolled delivery that is stilted, dull, mechanical, and boring.

It's tough to convince people that they shouldn't worry about being perfect in oral communications. One reason they set such a high standard for themselves is that they're afraid of becoming public targets. Remember, most businessmen got where they are in private rooms. They were very good, very skilled, and persuasive. But they didn't do it in public. Today, there's much more pressure on people in business to be public figures. The news media and the community expect more openness from executives today. Therefore, executives spend a great deal of time trying to appear as if they're not vulnerable, when in fact, if they appeared more human, more vulnerable, and didn't try to be perfect, they'd do a much better job at communications. I've seen people who are technically very good at speech and the audience goes out of the room yawning. I've seen people who don't have great voices, who even fumble a bit, but because they're committed to what they're saying and they're interesting, the audience goes out happy, saying, "I could have listened longer." Given a choice, the audience will always opt for the interesting but technically imperfect speaker over the one who's technically near perfect but boring.

VULNERABILITY

Ironically, strength comes from vulnerability. This is true in public speech as well as in interpersonal communications. In business, we're taught not to be vulnerable. We go in with a poker face, we sit a certain way, we have a so-called command presence. We have learned to be the leader in the rigid militaristic sense of the word. But imagine, as an alternative, that you toss a certain amount of your own vulnerability on the table. You're not frightened that you're going to be exposed or ruined or used unfairly. You choose instead to be open and candid. Because of your openness, other players feel more relaxed. Let me give you an example.

HIZZONER

In 1980, New York City Mayor Ed Koch appeared on one of those Sunday "newsmaker" programs in the aftermath of the city's financial crisis. Koch had spent three hundred thousand dollars to put up bike lanes in Manhattan. As it turned out, cars were driving in the bike lanes, endangering the bikers. Meanwhile, some bikers were running over pedestrians because the pedestrians didn't know the bike lanes were there or didn't understand how they worked. It was a mess. The mayor was coming up for reelection, and four or five journalists now had Koch cornered on this talk show. The whole purpose was to rip the mayor's skin off for the bike lanes and for spending money foolishly when the city was nearly broke. The trap was set. One reporter led off with "Mayor Koch, in light of the financial difficulties in New York City, how could you possibly justify wasting three hundred thousand dollars on bike lanes?" Cut to Koch. Tight close-up. Everybody was expecting a half-hour disaster. Koch smiled and he said, "You're right. It was a terrible idea." He went on, "I thought it would work. It didn't. It was one of the worst mistakes I ever made." And he stopped. Now nobody knew what to do. They had another twenty-six minutes of the program left. They all had prepared questions about the bike lanes, and so the next person feebly asked, "But, Mayor Koch, how could you do this?" And Mayor Koch said, "I already told you, it was stupid. I did a dumb thing. It didn't work." And he stopped again. Now there were twenty-five minutes left and nothing to ask him. It was brilliant.

Sometimes candor and vulnerability are the best answers. I thought to myself at the time, "This guy's going to get a heck of a lot of votes from doing this, because they're trying to beat him up and he's already admitted he blew it." Mayor Koch went on to receive both the Democratic and Republican endorsements for reelection.

ENERGY

In addition to showing a little vulnerability, using some energy can help you overcome fear, too. If you're energized and your heart's pumping a little bit, you won't black out. Gesturing helps to keep your energy up because physical movement burns off anxiety and helps pump the blood to the brain. When I work with clients, I try to get them to move a little when they speak, to gesture naturally. Not only does it counteract their fear, it also makes them look more dynamic. Just imagine our caveman friend Barney describing the hunt without gesturing. That would ruin a good story. Yet the modern "caveman," in his three-piece suit, has turned many an exciting report about a "hunt" for new business into a dull paper chase because he reads without energy from a text.

ROOTING FOR YOU

Audiences generally want the speaker to succeed. Part of the reason is that we can picture ourselves in the speaker's place, so we sympathize. Also, we don't want to be bored. Therefore, most audiences want to make the speaker comfortable in the hope that it will help the speaker perform better. We've all been in an audience when a speaker starts to wander, or his voice starts to quiver, or he forgets what to say and panics. It's clear he's in trouble and you pray that a trapdoor will open up and swallow him. Then you realize that he's got twenty minutes more of this agony to go through. When this happens, the audience begins to reflect the speaker. They begin to grip the arms of their chairs, clear their throats, look at the ceiling, and slide lower in their seats.

On the other hand, if the speaker gets up and appears to really know what he's doing—he's in charge, he's relaxed, he's comfortable—the audience begins to reflect that, too, and enjoys the speech. To a large extent, the first thing a speaker has to do is get all the attention off himself and deal with his topic. This helps make the audience comfortable. The comfort level of the audience begins with the speaker.

IF YOU FUMBLE

If you do goof up, which we all do, don't get worried. I once saw Walter Cronkite in person and he blew a few lines in his speech. He stopped, smiled, picked it up, and pulled out of it beautifully. It's important to have good grammar, but if we were to transcribe each word, some sentences would be grammatically correct and some wouldn't. That's okay as long as the audience understands what you mean. After all, if a guy comes up to you and says, "Stick 'em up," you don't look for the subject and the predicate. You look for your wallet.

A GOOD TRIP

The most dramatic example I ever saw of speaker comfort was what happened to one of my friends who was running for governor. He's a very nice, easygoing guy with a good sense of humor. His campaign was lagging and he was not getting much press coverage. He was set to speak at a legislative-correspondents dinner. The whole audience was made up of tough, professional reporters. On the way to the lectern, going up the stairs to the stage, he tripped and fell clear to his hands. He just got up, dusted himself off, and joked about it.

He said, "It's been so long since a reporter has listened to me, I got a little overanxious." The audience laughed and then applauded.

I later asked a newspaper reporter how the candidate did in his remarks. The reporter was somebody who didn't like his politics. She said, "On a one to ten, he got a ten." Then I asked another reporter. He said, "He got a nine."

Very few people literally "fall on their face" in front of a potentially hostile audience. This man did. But with his confident attitude and good humor, he ended up with rave reviews because he was able to relax the audience.

Some of the greatest communications challenges are faced when we are put in a position of leadership. In the next two chapters, we'll examine a critical aspect of leadership communication: dealing with the news media.

14
"MAKING IT" IN GRANDMA'S EYES

My grandmother was a sweet lady who loved me but could never figure out why, after I studied radio and TV in college, I couldn't fix her TV set. The guy down the street never went to college, but he fixed her set and charged her fifty dollars. I suspect that until she died in her eighties she figured I would eventually "make it" if I could just learn to fix her set. She never really knew what a producer did and she vaguely suspected I didn't have a real job. I had a lot of illness as a child, and my mother had to work to help support the family, which was unusual back in the 1940s and 1950s. Therefore I spent a great deal of time with my grandmother. Every Saturday we would go to the movies, and I think that gave me great interest in show business and the arts.

Grandma was a simple woman with little education but a strong sense of values. She was born before the turn of the century, and even though there were many advances in science, technology, and household conveniences during her lifetime, the greatest miracle in her life was television. She couldn't understand how all those people could get into that one little box. She watched Lawrence Welk religiously and knew about all of the families of the people on the show. The concept of television technology evaded her, though. She was lonely in her later years, and it really didn't matter about the technology as long as her friends were there when she pushed the button.

In 1964, I remember she was adamantly opposed to Barry Goldwater for president because she had heard that he was against TV. I never understood this but eventually questioned her at great length. She swore that she read in the paper that he was against television. I think she thought Barry Goldwater, if elected president, would personally come up on her porch and take her TV set away. I found out later that Barry Goldwater had said he was against TVA—Tennessee Valley Authority. Grandma never heard the *A* and disliked Goldwater until she died.

THE MIRACLE

I once knew a television sales manager who couldn't describe the miracle of television, either. So when people asked him what he did for a living, he said, "I sell pictures that fly through the air." That may be the best description I've ever heard. Actually, because television is a miracle, we act the way we do in the presence of all miracles—we change our behavior. Because there is something mysterious about it, it's intimidating. And consequently, we often act unlike ourselves when a television camera is present. I still can't repair a TV set, but I often think television has done so much good for people that I hope they have television in heaven. And I hope to God that at least one TV repairman led a good enough life to make it up there, too, so he can fix Grandma's TV set.

GUILTY TILL PROVEN INNOCENT

Today, people come to me for a different type of TV repair. I often "fix" the programs themselves or the people who are going to appear on them.

The typical situation involves a company about to be featured on a TV news program. Since nobody ever wins a journalism award for reporting on the good things companies do, the chances are that my client is facing allegations that will ultimately prove to be somewhere between the truth and a hysterical rumor. In the interest of fair play and equal time, the journalist on the story has offered to interview a company spokesperson. The interview will take two hours and will be edited down to thirty seconds or less (although the interviewer doesn't tell him that). Unfortunately, in today's world of media, if you get a negative story, many people assume you must be guilty of something. That's what so many companies fear—and with good reason.

Mark Twain said it best: "A lie can travel halfway around the world while the truth is putting on its shoes."

GIRDING FOR BATTLE

The chairman of the company is sitting in my New York studio. He's asking me where to begin when Geraldo Rivera or his regional equivalent comes crashing into the boardroom with his kamikaze camera crew, equipped with zoom lenses, glaring lights, and microphones. The reporter, of course, wants an explanation—preferably a confession of guilt—in time for the six o'clock news.

The fact that the executive is in my office says a lot about the communication requirements of a business leader. Today, executives had better be prepared to meet the press, especially if a crisis catapults their company onto the front page or the evening news. Years ago, Ralph Nader came out with his first book, *Unsafe at Any Speed*, an attack on American cars, including the Corvair. I scheduled Nader for a TV appearance. It seemed only fair to get somebody from General Motors to refute Nader's allegations. I called the company and asked for an executive spokesperson. The company wouldn't even send someone from the public relations department. It played ostrich, refusing to acknowledge that I, Nader, or the book even existed.

Businesses today may be as wary as ever of the news media, but most companies understand that if they remain silent during a controversy, they will be presumed guilty by the press and, probably, by the public. Although some companies (such as Mobil Oil) believed early on in the value of actively engaging their critics, many people in business still wait until news coverage escalates to kangaroo-court proportions before they finally defend themselves.

NO PLACE TO HIDE

There is no hiding from the media today. In the United States in 1994, there were 1,512 television stations, 11,558 radio stations, 12,513 newspapers, 12,136 periodicals, and 11,214 cable-operating systems.

Every hour of every day, these news and information-gathering media need to fill an insatiable "new hole" with stories and reports. No one is safe from the relentless scrutiny of some critic somewhere, who uses the news media to publicize—and, sometimes, to sensationalize—rumors and allegations. For better or worse, the news media have become like lawyers. They'll take on almost any case, often without enough consideration of its merits. Even the Girl Scouts have been attacked these days for "exploiting child labor" when little girls go door-to-door selling cookies!

The late pop artist Andy Warhol once made what sounded like an off-the-wall prediction about all this. He said that in the future, everyone will be famous for fifteen minutes—because eventually every American will be interviewed on TV. If you watch the evening news or pick up a newspaper, Andy Warhol's seemingly outrageous forecast appears to be coming true. In the past, people in business could be assured that their visibility would be confined within the company. Today, with the news media probing everywhere, it is increasingly likely that even a middle manager will at least be quoted in a trade journal. The most senior executives are almost bound to appear on a cable TV news program or a radio show. As you rise to more prominence in your company, the odds increase that your exposure will include being on a network or local TV news program and being quoted on the pages of major business news publications.

If the idea of appearing on TV in a confrontational format scares the hell out of you, you're not alone. There are any number of how-to books that can give you useful advice about how to appear on a radio or television program or do a print interview. What I want to do is talk about the goals of the media versus the goals of the person interviewed and give some examples where helpful principles apply. I recommend several tactics, but the emphasis is on strategy.

THE JOURNALIST'S JOB

Before we even begin to discuss strategies for communicating effectively with the news media, we should take a look at the people in the media and get a feel for what journalists' jobs are all about.

In his book *Reporting*, Lou Cannon, *The Washington Post*'s White House correspondent, writes that many people become journalists "because they seek to have some social impact on the world." He adds that "the reporter's view that he is performing a sacred calling can cloak him with an annoying self-righteousness about his mission which ordinary Americans find disturbing. Out of this attitude of mission sometimes arises an insensitivity and a belief that a reporter is entitled to ask anyone anything at any time."[15] While many actually believe that a reporter should do exactly that, we have all seen examples of questionable taste, if not questionable ethics, exhibited by reporters.

Hostility toward the press is nothing new. In a book called *How True* by Thomas Griffith, former editor of *Time* and *Life* magazines, there is a quote from a nineteenth-century etiquette book. It advises the well-bred reader that it is improper to order a newspaperman kicked down the stairs simply because he has chosen to make his living in a disagreeable manner.[16]

A more balanced and contemporary view is that reporters are human, therefore they have biases. But most good reporters work at being fair. Their interpretation of what's fair, however, is sometimes in question. Many journalists seem to want to tear down the social order or institutions. They want to raise questions about or challenges to the establishment. I think those challenges and questions are good, and I believe in the journalists' right to ask any question they want. I also believe in people not answering certain questions if they feel they needn't or shouldn't. I believe that people have a right not to appear guilty simply because they have chosen to ignore or deflect a question.

I don't subscribe to the theory that every journalist is out to "get" business—to find a scandal, whether one exists or not. I do believe, however, that there should be a healthy skepticism on both sides: on the part of the interviewer and of the interviewee.

If the executive understands that the press does not exist to serve as his public relations arms, and the executive is prepared to live with that, then the company should establish a policy whereby, except in highly unusual circumstances, its officials make themselves available to reporters. On the other hand, I know one major Fortune 500 company whose policy is never to talk to the press. When the press calls, the company says they've moved. The effect of the company's press paranoia is suspicion and hatred by the press. It will eventually result in a media relations disaster for the company. There are other cases where, in my judgment, a business is too open to the press and becomes a whipping boy. A company must respect the journalist's goals and simultaneously mind its own business. If company officials can contribute to a story in a manner that will not be detrimental to the shareholders, fine.

TWO VIEWS

Journalists tell me they are sometimes tough on business because business hides from them and they figure there must be something to hide. Businesses tell me that the reason they don't talk to the press is that reporters always print the negative and never the positive. There is some truth to both arguments. Business should sponsor more forums or behind-the-scenes seminars so that business and the press can get to know each other. That doesn't mean that the press is never going to be negative, but the press needs to know what is driving the business world. Business also needs to understand that the goal of the press is to gather information, and the press has the right to report negative news when it finds it. Sometimes the press is looking for information to support a story or premise, sometimes they're just gathering specific data, and sometimes they're "fishing."

The first responsibility of the reporter is to his job. If he quotes some vice president in a negative way and it costs that man his career, it may deeply bother the reporter. He may even lose sleep over it. But it won't stop the reporter from using it.

ONLY KIDDING

One executive came to us after he was quoted in the press and his company's stock went down three points the next day. He had said some things to a reporter that he thought were "off the record" and they ended up in print. I tell my clients, "The only thing off the record is what you don't say." There are some journalists who will respect off the record and there are some who won't. In general, it's better not to gamble on this issue.

That executive I mentioned had just been appointed president of a research and manufacturing subsidiary of a large corporation. He agreed to spend a day with a male reporter from a major newspaper so that the reporter could write a personality profile of him. Together, they toured the laboratories, the plant, and the offices of the subsidiary. They became friendly and comfortable with one another. This executive was a "good ole boy" Southerner who enjoyed wisecracking and had an eye for a pretty lady. At one point he passed a very well endowed young secretary, and he poked the reporter in the ribs, winked, and said, "My God, will you look at the build on that little bit of heaven?"

The reporter smiled and said nothing. At the end of the day, the reporter was about to drive to the airport. During the casual parting conversation, the reporter asked the executive, "How come you're still commuting between company headquarters in Los Angeles and the plant here?" Again, the executive winked and answered, "Because the nightlife is better in Los Angeles." It was a throwaway remark. The executive thought the interview was over and he was just talking to a "friend."

When the profile of the executive appeared in the newspaper, it praised him as smart and tough. But it also alluded to his arrogance, sexism, and other off-putting traits. The article ended with a quote denigrating the local nightlife.

Not only did all hell break loose with some stockholders, but the executive also was reprimanded within his company—to his face and behind his back. In a rage, he called the reporter. "You screwed me!" he yelled. Coolly, the reporter replied, "Before you get your jockey shorts in a bundle, just remember that I let you off light. I could've—but didn't—quote you about the build on that little bit of heaven."

The reporter hung up. Two days later, the executive was in my office for our first session together. "That son of a bitch," he whined, "treed me like a hound dog."

ON OR OFF?

What's on the record? What's off the record? The problem is, there are no rules. There are many fine reporters who will distinguish for you between (1) material they'll use only with your name; (2) material they'll take on "background" without specific attribution; and (3) material they'll just use for their own better understanding of the issues. Unfortunately, for many reporters, distinguishing between these categories and remembering (or honoring) confidentiality agreements can get hazy, especially when a story becomes "hot" or when it's a "scoop" and the reporter is under a crushing deadline.

If the material is interesting, it's best to go on record or not pique the reporter's interest. A lot of younger journalists believe that the public interest is best served when they alone decide what counts as off the record. Many, many people have been caught off guard with that new theory. President Reagan's remark that "we begin bombing [the Russians] in five minutes" was made as a joke when a recording engineer asked him to say something so he could check Reagan's voice level prior to the president's weekly radio address. By agreement with reporters, anything said during that routine test is off the record. For literally centuries, presidents have joked with reporters during these kinds of mutually acknowledged, undocumented moments. Presidents Roosevelt and Kennedy, in particular, had gentlemen's agreements with the press about speaking off the record. But some news organizations broke the understanding and played up Reagan's "bombing" remark in a big way. If Reagan had realized that the off-the-record agreement would not be honored, do you think he would have made the joke? Even less explosive comments can cause problems. So if you have wisecracking instincts, it's best to keep them in check around the media. Reagan is a professional. He should have known better.

SELLING OTHERS OUT

A good friend of mine who is a reporter told me about an experience he had at an editor's conference. A grizzled senior editor leaned over his desk, looked at all the young reporters, and snarled, "You know why so many of you are going to get divorced and a lot of you will become alcoholics? Because you are now in the business of selling people out. Your job is to get close to your sources, get as much out of them as you can, and then print it, and don't worry about them. You say you're defending the public interest. Your job is to stick it to the guy who trusted you enough to spill his guts to you. And if you can't handle that, get out of the business now!"

That's depressing, and it's only one cynical man's viewpoint. But there are people who subscribe to it. And the essence of what he said is all too often true. It's comments like these that cause many to say the media is a jungle.

NO LIES, NO APOLOGIES

At least part of any good reporter's job is to get people to talk openly and freely. The methods he or she employs are uniquely his or her own. A reporter can bother, flatter, intimidate, cajole, humor, beg, and use a myriad of other techniques to get you to talk. That does not mean that you shouldn't talk to the press; it does mean you should be aware of what's going on at all times. The main thing to keep in mind is that reporters are under absolutely no obligation to print what you say, but they can if they choose to, and you are under absolutely no obligation to tell them something that is damaging to you or your business. Until you know exactly what you want to say and have all the information you need, beware of any reporter who tells you he is doing a story on you and/or your company, and that it will be better for you if you talk to him. First, that's an implied threat. Second, a good way to translate what he's saying is that he simply doesn't have enough information to do the story without your corroboration. Third, he may be on a witch hunt. Fourth, he may have damaging information and he wants you to incriminate yourself. If it appears the reporter intends to be unfair to begin with, he's not going to play fair later. Business goes wrong when it turns down reasonable requests for interviews, reasonable information requested by the press, and reasonable access when there's no need to hide.

The press is not going to like what I have to say next: I have never known of a person's being fired because he or she refused to talk to the press and turned it over to his or her public relations department. I have known people who were fired because they gave unauthorized information to the press. If you can, give reporters everything they need to do the story. If you can't, don't jeopardize your career because somebody is putting intense pressure on you at the moment. If you do speak, never lie. If you don't speak, never apologize. Most of the good reporters I know will respect you if you say, "Look, I'd like to tell you more, but this is difficult for me and I'm not authorized to speak in this area. I don't want to create a false impression by giving simplistic answers, and you'll just have to respect the fact that I choose not to speak on this topic at this time." The reporter may still want to come back to you later to confirm something, or use you as a future source, so it's unlikely he'll cut off all communications at that point. If he does, what have you lost?

Don't ever be cowed or pushed because a reporter is on a deadline. That's his problem, not yours. If you don't have your facts straight, or you haven't had time to think about what you want to say, don't live by his artificial deadline. "Urgent" or "important" are words the reporter is using to describe a situation which exists in his life. There's a tendency to believe that the situation truly is urgent and to fall into the trap of trying to help the reporter meet his deadline. You have an obligation to try to provide the reporter with the factual information when it's possible. And in fact, over a period of time, if you're consistent, the reporter will come to regard you as a credible source and understand that, when you choose not to give him something, it's not a personal affront. The bottom line is, you have a job, and he has a job: They are not the same job. Don't confuse them. There is absolutely no reason for hostility toward reporters as a group. Don't ever try to manipulate the press to gain personal publicity. It will almost always backfire. There's an old saying in life: "Be careful of what you want, because you're liable to get it." In this regard I would say, "Be careful what you say; they'll probably print it."

15
MEDIA TACTICS: SCORING ON DEFENSE

Basketball and football coaches have a saying: "You can't score on defense—get the ball."

With the media, make no mistake. You are always on defense, but if you do it right, you can occasionally score.

First recognize that the media has nothing to lose by interviewing you. On the other hand, you or those you represent could lose.

How, then, can you prepare yourself to deal with the news media? What are the strategies and techniques for handling journalists? I will summarize the highlights of what we tell our clients. To begin with, don't ever take a phone call from a reporter you don't know. First, tell the reporter, or have your secretary tell him, that you'll get back to him. You need time to check out who the reporter is, what he could possibly want, and why he might want it. You need to think and compose yourself. Mistakes are made when people rush into media interviews without really analyzing the intent of the reporter. What the reporter tells you may or may not be totally true. I've met few reporters who will actually lie, but many who have hidden agendas.

Even Laurence A. Tisch, president and chief executive officer of CBS Inc., admitted to *The Wall Street Journal* on March 20,

1987, that negative reporting by the news media about his budget and staff cutbacks had "broken" his company's image. "I've lost a certain confidence in the press, I must say," Tisch said in a tape-recorded interview. "I won't be as ready just to talk to people over the telephone."

One executive was sent to me after he had embarrassed his company by giving a candid interview to a reporter who identified himself as being with *The New York Times*. My client naively assumed the reporter was legitimate, and he took the call without verifying the caller's credentials. The "reporter" turned out to be a free-lancer calling from a pay phone. The article, which misquoted the client and maligned the company, ended up in an underground scandal sheet. Pieces of the article later surfaced in establishment publications.

Once you've checked the reporter out, you'll find that most of the time, he has no ill intent: He simply wants information. He's been assigned a story. If you cooperate and give the reporter facts which are interesting enough to be quoted, your side of the story may at least be heard. It may not appear with the background and explanation you'd ideally want, but you'll probably fare better than you would by not responding.

Never go into a media interview unprepared. Never try to "wing it." Instead, discuss the interview in advance with a public relations professional, a media consultant, or other trusted counsel. If you can, review prior newsclips or program tapes to get a feel for the reporter's point of view. Anticipate likely questions—think through your replies. Reverse roles: If you were the journalist or the audience for the story, what questions or issues would you want addressed? (Be objective and tough on yourself.) Consider: Who is my audience? What do I want my audience to remember (or do) as a result of what I say? Why am I being interviewed (purpose) and why should my audience listen to me? (Address their concerns and bear in mind that the public viewpoint may differ from the corporate perspective.) How will I organize and deliver my remarks?

Think it through and invest sufficient time. There is no substitute for thorough preparation and rehearsal.

Have an agenda of three major points you want to discuss in the interview, and plan to work those points in sometime during your conversation with the reporter. The most common mistake made by people who are interviewed is that they wait for the reporter to ask questions which will trigger their agenda points. That may never happen. Jon once trained a dermatologist who was preparing for a media tour to discuss a new skin product. In one of the practice interviews, Jon sidetracked her into focusing for five minutes on how overexposure to the sun can damage the skin. She didn't once mention the name of the new product—although it was related to sun and skin problems—and suddenly her "time was up." When you're interviewed by a reporter, you shouldn't just be a backboard for his or her questions. You should gently take enough control, at times, to get *your* points across.

WHO SETS THE AGENDA?

Remember, the medium determines the message. Print interviews allow you time to explain. But radio and TV interviews require "headline" answers—bulleted "highlights" delivered in a few short, vivid sentences. The average radio or TV quote by an individual is edited down to fifteen or twenty seconds— about the time you would need to read this paragraph aloud.

A media interview is give-and-take. It can't run along parallel tracks that never meet.

Reporter's agenda *(series of questions)*		Your agenda *(point of view)*

Reporters and the people they interview become at odds when either party tries to follow only his own agenda and refuses to address the other person's needs.

Ask yourself: How can I build a bridge from the reporter's agenda to my own agenda? You can do this successfully if your agenda consists of points made interesting and newsworthy with the support of facts, illustrations, and examples. Be responsive to the journalist's questions, but don't give away the store. You are not obliged to reveal confidential information. However, don't dismiss a question by saying, "No comment." If you must withhold information, explain in a nice way that the facts are proprietary. Then explain why (for example, "Our competitors would love to know that—which is why I can't elaborate"). Next, offer alternative information, if appropriate. Above all, in your attitude, avoid giving the impression that you are stonewalling.

$Q = A + 1$ is a formula my associate, Jon Kraushar, learned from a friend, human resources consultant Don Teff. When asked a question (Q), reply briefly and directly with an answer (A). Then, if it will help, add a point or points ($+1$), preferably from your agenda. For example, one of my clients, a congressman, was asked by a reporter, "You were pressured by the big chemical companies not to introduce that legislation, weren't you?" The congressman answered, "I met with everyone involved in the issue, including the environmentalists, the consumer groups, and the companies." Then he added ($+1$), "Based on these discussions, all the parties agreed that the industry would set new standards rather than Congress passing a law."

Accept the fact that reporters are, first and foremost, after a story, although not necessarily the story you want to give them. Do not be hostile or condescending toward a reporter. Don't threaten to withdraw advertising because a story upsets you. You can sometimes head off problems with a story before it is published by asking a reporter if you can review his text to insure accuracy of your quotes and facts about the company. Some journalists allow you to check substance but will become angry if you request changes in writing style. That offends the reporter's pride and ego. You can request a prior story review, but if the reporter objects, you're probably better off not pushing the issue. There are two principles here: (1) If you don't ask, you can't get, but (2) after you've asked, be sensitive to how far you can go.

Hostility is a no-win strategy with the press—they have the last word. But friendliness is no guarantee of good coverage either. You won't lose points by being nice. But remember, being friendly with a reporter does not make the reporter "your friend."

On radio and TV, your air of decisiveness (style/delivery) is as important as your substance (content/words). Be friendly, be brief, be direct, and be positive.

Unless you're being interviewed for highly technical journals, avoid jargon. Speak plainly. Use examples and illustrations that enable the average person to understand you. Use laymen's terms.

PLAIN SPEAKING

The late business writer Bill Hunter once compiled some of the more outrageous double-talk and euphemisms used in business. These are real examples: One company avoided the word "loss" in its annual report by referring to "net profits revenue deficiency." You'd think a papermaking company got its product from trees, but the term it used was "reforestation unit." When the money in some banks doesn't grow on reforestation units, it's referred to as "nonperforming loans." Aren't those the kind that aren't repaid? Today, you don't get fired from a job—you're "outplaced." Funds aren't stolen from companies—they're "misappropriated." Even lies have become "disinformation."[17] The best advice on jargon? Downscale it. Disinvest in it. Outplace it.

A SEARCH-AND-DESTROY MISSION

Also, remember to stay composed—at all times. A reporter may provoke you with the hope that you will blow up and leak sensitive information or blurt out a controversial quote. Journalistic techniques to unveil colorful information include badgering you and asking you the same basic question over and over. Don't take these strategies personally! (It's the reporter's job.) Occasionally, you'll run into a reporter who appears to be on a search-and-destroy mission. Once the interview has started, there is little you can do except fasten your seat belt, stay calm, smile, and give very short answers.

Always be aware, especially on TV, of where the audience's sympathy lies. If a reporter is bullying you, the viewers at home may start to root for you. The audience, not the reporter, is your constituency. Reporters believe they serve the public. So, often in their style and manner, they feel that anything is fair. Remember, you bring a different standard of fairness to the interview, and the audience may bring an altogether different, third standard of fairness. Actually, the audience has a pretty good idea of what is fair. The audience often will be on your side in an interview with the press if you can't escalate your emotions to hostility. Take ABC-TV's Sam Donaldson, for instance. He does not answer to anyone except the network. He has nothing to lose by being a little hostile. He goads you to the point of exasperation with his hectoring. He wants you to lose your temper and say something extreme so he'll get his headline. When you hear a pickup in the reporter's tone and volume and rhythm of interrogation, your response should generally be friendlier, quieter, and slower. That cues the audience that you're the reasonable party and the reporter is just trying to provoke you. Exercise the law of inverse proportions. The more inflammatory the journalist, the cooler you should be.

Donaldson became the personification of the tough reporter by hounding President Reagan. The president once had a chance to even the score with Donaldson—in his usual, kidding way—when he addressed the annual dinner of the White House Correspondents' Association in April of 1986. The president said, "At my last press conference I thought that gimmick of wearing a red dress to get my attention went a little too far. Nice try, Sam." The press roared with laughter.

CBS anchorman Dan Rather uses an analogy to describe what he sees as the appropriate relationship between the news media and those they interview. He says that journalists shouldn't be expected to act like friendly lapdogs, rolling over for news sources, accepting information exactly as sources provide it without question. Nor, says Rather, should journalists be killer-instinct attack dogs, indiscriminately going for the throats of people they pursue on stories and trying to destroy those they interview, professionally and personally. The ideal role of the journalist, according to Rather, is the watchdog—alert, wary, sniffing out trespassers, and protective of the public interest.

I agree with Rather in principle. However, it's important to note that one person's watchdog (alertness) is another person's attack dog (assault).

I've already discussed executives or companies who stonewall the press. But just as potentially destructive are journalists who "stone" the people they interview, just for the confrontational drama the clash provides. Many media interviews are like bullfights. The matador (the journalist) tries to control the ring, and he certainly holds the ultimate weapons (when his reportage is made public). Nonetheless, it is possible for the bull (you) to win occasionally—or at least not get killed.

GOLDEN RULES

One of the most dramatic examples of this happened in 1982, when Mike Wallace of "60 Minutes" called the Adolph Coors Company in Golden, Colorado, to do an interview with owners Joe and Bill Coors. Coors had been accused of union busting and discriminatory practices. At first, Joe and Bill Coors were reluctant to do the interview. But after meeting with their public relations people, they decided to open the doors and let "60 Minutes" in. The owners then spent a good deal of time and money preparing for the "60 Minutes" interview. They felt the facts were on their side and they wanted an opportunity to present those facts to the American people. In essence, they did everything we talked about in this chapter, including rehearsing the actual interview with the most likely questions that Wallace would ask.

By the time the session actually took place, the Coors brothers were calm, relaxed, and ready. Not only were they able to answer Mike Wallace's questions, but they got several of their own positive points into the interview as well. The "60 Minutes" segment which eventually aired turned out to be a major public relations boost for Coors. It was so strongly favorable that Coors bought the noncommercial rights to the "60 Minutes" segment for forty thousand dollars and made more than four hundred copies to send to Coors distributors and local service clubs all over America. This never could have happened if Coors didn't have a strong case. But the important element here is that the owners took it seriously, did what they had to do, and probably were better prepared for the actual interview than the "60 Minutes" crew.

REPOSITIONING

In many press interviews, reporters will use loaded words in a question. Don't legitimize these words by repeating them in the answer. Recast language or issues into factual terms. In effect, you *reposition* the negative premise of the question.

For example, if a reporter characterizes your actions as "corrupt, irresponsible, malicious, and injurious to the public welfare," you should not say, "We are *not* corrupt, irresponsible, malicious, and injurious to the public welfare." All you're doing then is repeating the charges, which will reinforce and help people remember the words of indictment even more. Instead, you might say, "We've answered our critics by . . ." and then describe positive, concrete actions you've taken.

Whenever there's a loaded question like that, you might also smile and point out that the question is loaded by saying, "Well, obviously, you have a strong opinion against us in this, and let me try to give you the facts." And then go into your litany.

Our advice to both our political and business clients is to develop three levels or "tiers" of an answer to the most nettlesome questions they could be asked by a reporter. The first level, tier A, is a one- or two-sentence summary of your position. If a reporter wants elaboration, you are ready with tier

B, a concrete example to back up that summary, plus a little more detail. Most reporters won't need more than two levels to an answer, but if need be, you should be ready with tier C, a further elaboration using another supporting statement.

If a reporter wants to push you past C, loop back to your tier A reply. This system keeps you solidly on your position, regardless of how aggressively a reporter wants to push you to an indiscreet reply. Here's a hypothetical example:

REPORTER: (to company chairman) Your salary and bonus are outrageous and exorbitant, especially compared to what your employees are paid.

CHAIRMAN: (tier A reply) My pay is in line with the compensation for the chairmen of similar-sized and similar-performing companies. As you know, I don't set my compensation. It's set by a group of professionals who look at many factors.

REPORTER: But it's like extorting the shareholders. I mean, a million dollars a year. And your company *lost* money last year.

CHAIRMAN: (tier B reply) My compensation is based on longer-term rates of return than one year. Our average rate of return on common stock during my five years as chairman is 22 percent, double the five-year average for the industry.

REPORTER: But don't you think you're still overpaid?

CHAIRMAN: (tier C reply) I'm paid based on my long-term ability to manage the company and the challenges of the job. For example, the right fielder for the Angels is paid $1.4 million a year. You're compensated according to the standards and practices of your business.

REPORTER: But you haven't answered my question. Aren't you overpaid?

CHAIRMAN: (looping back to tier A, smiling) Well, as I said before, it's what chairmen of similar-sized and similar-performing companies earn.

REPORTER: I still think it's too much. . . . (pause)

CHAIRMAN: (silence—don't get sucked in)

A RULE OF THUMB

As you can extrapolate from this example, it's also a good rule of thumb that the tougher the questions, the shorter your answers should be. Many people foul themselves up in interviews by giving rambling replies. Either they end up sounding as though they're "protesting too much" or they say something inaccurate or indiscreet in an attempt to be responsive to the premise of the question.

The premises of questions from journalists are sometimes objectionable themselves—or hypothetical. You have no obligation to legitimize a hypothetical or false premise.

The savvy former director of the Arms Control and Disarmament Agency, Kenneth Adelman, once appeared on a Sunday morning national news program. A reporter asked Adelman if the Soviet Union might be using Cuba at that very moment to build up arms supplies and then threaten the East Coast of the United States. Adelman said, "No." That's all. The reporter didn't know what to do after that. There was silence. Silence is an enemy on television, a medium where advertisers can pay up to $950,000 for a minute of airtime. So the reporter scrambled around for his next question.

Whether it's a TV, radio, or print interview, say what you have to say, then stop. It's the reporter's problem to come up with the next question. Whenever you can, frame your answers in the context of "the public interest," which reporters believe they protect and represent. For example, rather than focusing on the return on investment of a new product—as you might at a board of directors meeting—focus with a reporter on the ways the new product will save some consumers time or money or otherwise improve their lives. Answer one question at a time. If you are unsure of the answer, admit it candidly. Say what you can, but don't fudge. And don't lie. It will come back to haunt you.

Match your facial expression to the seriousness of the message. Use gestures—don't be a stiff. Look your interviewer in the eye. Shifty eyes signal discomfort or guilt.

DRESS

On TV or in public, don't let your wardrobe overwhelm your words. What you have to say is more important than what you're wearing. In general, dress conservatively—nothing gaudy or loud, whether it be a suit, makeup for women, or accessories ranging from ties to jewelry. If you're in doubt, here are some rules of thumb. Whether you're wearing a two- or three-piece outfit (vests tend to bunch up when you sit, especially if you're overweight), only one item should be patterned and the pattern should be subtle. The other items should be solid shades, neither too dark nor too light. TV cameras are supposed to be able to adjust to extreme darks and lights, but they can't adjust completely. For example, a black person dressed all in black against a dark background will practically disappear on screen. Same for a white person dressed in white against a light background. The solution is to wear navy blue, grey, and other dark (but not funereal black) suits. Shirts should be lighter than suits, but neither solid black nor stark white. The pattern you choose to wear should be muted, because bold patterns create a "bleeding," "smudgy," or "shimmering eel" effect on TV. The pattern "trails" just behind when the wearer turns or moves. The TV's lines of resolution just can't keep up with a bold, moving pattern. The same rule of "less is more" applies to shoes, jewelry, and various adornments. Stay away from boots, heavy makeup, or jangling jewelry, unless you're a gypsy fortune-teller. On TV, men will need some makeup to cut the glare of the bright lights or to cover facial blemishes. The same for women. Men may need light makeup to soften a heavy beard or to hold down the glare from a bald head. Too much makeup is a disaster. The rule is, you should not see makeup. Ask to see a close-up shot of yourself on the studio or control room monitor. If you see patches or streaks of makeup, refuse to go on until it's fixed. But be persistent in a nice way.

CROWD CONTROL

In the confusion of informal hallway interviews—where there are as many as ten or twelve reporters pressing around you, pushing microphones toward you, and shouting questions—you can still bear down on the central issue, as developed for your TV appearances, if you are well prepared. You can also try to set the pace. If the questions are flying thick and fast and a commotion is occurring, you can usually quiet the reporters by opening your mouth and uttering a few words, such as "Let me just say . . ." The reporters will hush in order to hear your words. Once the quiet sets in, you can deliver your prepared pitch. When you pause, the questions will begin again.

If you're besieged by a flock of reporters (let's say on the steps of a court building), try to control the situation by selecting a single question to which you will respond. Look at the reporter who asked the question. Ignore the cameras and microphones surrounding you and speak to the questioner. Try to come in "under" the tone and volume of the questioner, speaking more calmly. If you shout excitedly, the TV viewer may decide that you sound defensive and are therefore guilty.

One of the techniques that I have occasionally advised clients to use is that if a reporter asks a really tough question, respond with an equally tough question. Here's a hypothetical example. Somebody asks, "Why did you vote against the environment?" You might reply, "Are you talking about House bill #135 that was part of the amendment to the EPA Superfund bill, or are you talking about the Baxter-Sawyer bill, which is in the conference committee now and which would allow a special fund to be set up by 1990 to handle toxic waste cleanup at sites determined to be a hazard by the EPA and substantiated by community standards?" The reporter's eyes will tell you quickly if he knows what he's doing or if he'll retreat and leave you alone. In many cases, he's just trying to provoke you. If his eyes roll around like pinballs, his knowledge of the issue is probably a mile wide and an inch deep. This technique can buy you time. Ask the question in a very friendly, good-natured way. You don't have to do it with hostility. You just say, "I need to clarify the point before I answer."

If you're able to smile at a time like this, make sure it's a natural one. If smiling comes hard, concentrate on listening to your interrogators, composing your sentence structure, and choosing specific words for your responses.

A TV DUEL

On a television program in the early 1970s, I witnessed one of the worst examples of someone who was totally unaware of the audience's sympathy and of the dynamics of hostility. In this case, it was a debate on a pollution issue. On one side was a puffed-up, pompous corporate executive. On the other side was a long-haired, earnest, but somewhat scruffy consumer advocate. The typecasting was classic TV: the "robber baron" versus the "hippie." The executive and the consumer activist began arguing, and the moderator went back and forth. Finally, the activist raised his voice to the corporate executive and said, "It's because of people like you that we can't breathe." The executive got angry, exasperated, and red in the face. Without thinking, he shouted back, "Young man, there are more important things than breathing!" A hush came over the set and everyone looked stunned, especially the executive. He realized he'd been provoked into making a ridiculous and extreme statement, absurd to everyone.

The news media often try to move you to extreme positions. They try to show both sides of issues as if all issues had only two sides. TV is a time medium. Black and white issues make for clear-cut controversy. The time restrictions and space limitations (plus the short attention span of the audience) make simplification the imperative of the media. They label you as being on the right or the wrong side, liberal or conservative, up or down. They try to move you with their questioning to the most extreme possible position so that they can get a "good" quote. If you ever dare agree with your opponent, the producers will not invite you back because you failed to provide the necessary "drama" of controversy. Of course, they won't say that. They'll just throw away your phone number.

In some cases, a reporter might hold his microphone under your chin too long, for a few extra "beats" after you have finished. Perhaps he doesn't realize that your statement is complete, and he expects you to continue. If the microphone lingers and the camera keeps rolling, simply restate your main theme. Sum it up. Be a stuck record. It's better to repeat than to dilute your story with what could be viewed as an indecisive fade-out. The tape editor at the studio will tighten the segment by trimming the repetitious dialogue. The same principle holds true in a print interview. Don't give in to pressure to go beyond the bounds of your position.

When you're appearing on TV, don't look around for the monitor, the camera crew, or other production staff. Let the equipment play to you. Don't play to the equipment. Don't worry about finding the right camera to look into. It's the job of the director and/or camera operator to find you. If the interview is outside of a television studio—in the "field"—and you're near people you know, don't look at them. Stay focused on the interviewer, even when listening. Always bear in mind that you may be on, even though you're not talking.

Also, recognize that any time you are in the presence of a newsperson, the conversation is fair game for the record. Jimmy Carter's famous confession that he sometimes had lust in his heart for women other than his wife was uttered to a *Playboy* magazine journalist as he was leaving Carter's home at the conclusion of the formal interview.

Even Mike Wallace, big-game hunter of the unguarded moment, got caught in this snare. As recounted on the op-ed page of *The Wall Street Journal* by TV critic Daniel Henninger in March of 1981, Wallace

> was interviewing a banker in San Diego about an alleged home-improvement fraud involving mainly blacks and Hispanics, who supposedly had signed contracts they couldn't understand, which eventually led to foreclosures on their home mortgages.
>
> The bank hired a film crew of its own to record the interview with Mr. Wallace. The bank's crew apparently left its recorder running during a break in the CBS interview, and the tape has Mr. Wallace saying, in reply to a question about why the black and Hispanic customers would have signed their contracts, "They're probably too busy eating their watermelon and tacos."

When the *Los Angeles Times* got wind of this indiscretion and reported it, there was at least a minor uproar from reporters and others about Wallace's "racially disparaging joke." Wallace ultimately pleaded "no bias," admitting that over time he'd privately told jokes about many ethnic groups but that his record "speaks for itself."

Henninger added, "Needless to say, this has to be the most deliciously lip-smacking bit of irony to pop out of the oven in a long time. Here we have the dogcatcher cornered. The lepidopterist pinned. The preacher in *flagrante delicto*. This is the fellow who has imputed all manner of crimes against social goodness to a long lineup of businessmen and bureaucrats. From here on out, all future victims of Mr. Wallace can take some small comfort in knowing that although they may stand exposed as goof-offs, thieves, and polluters, *he's* the guy who made the crack about the watermelons and tacos."

I know Mike Wallace, and in my opinion he is absolutely not a bigot. Quite the opposite, he is a champion of human rights, but he's human like everybody else. And we've all been guilty of saying things to friends in what we consider to be a private situation that might be disparaging to certain groups. As a matter of fact, it's quite normal for reporters and producers to engage in cynical dialogue. Of course, most executives feel —and correctly so—that if it had been them, or if it had been a politician who made that crack, it would have been news for two weeks and possibly could have ended a person's career. Some reporters did report Mike Wallace's comments, but it was not pursued and, therefore, was quickly forgotten.

I've had clients ask me if they should go on "60 Minutes." I usually tell them that if they are near retirement, have a golden parachute, and wish to go out in a blaze of glory, that is probably a good way to do it. Otherwise I don't advise them to do TV programs that are extensively edited. There are too many techniques that they are unaware of. The truth, as I said before, is that they will be interviewed for two hours and the network will use their most controversial eighteen seconds. Those seconds could be remarks out of context or could be the one moment they lose their cool. The primary goal of a program like this is to get ratings.

Nonetheless, I was once interviewed by "60 Minutes." I consented to the interview because I know the tricks and guerrilla tactics of journalists. I have worked in news. The person interviewing me either was trying to relax me or thought he'd get me to open up in some way in an unguarded moment. He ordered his crew to take a break. But I noticed that, while the crew locked their recording gear in place and drifted away, the camera lenses were uncapped and pointed at me. I heard the faint whir of the camera motor and I knew it was still on. The trick didn't work, so they officially continued the interview.

If executives want to do the "Today Show" or "Good Morning America" or the "CBS Morning Program," which are live or live on tape, they have a fair shot at saying what they want to say and being sure that it remains intact. If they do an extensively edited show, they are taking their chances.

When speaking to the press, you have to get used to repeating your story to different reporters while maintaining your energy and freshness. Some journalists (print or broadcast) want to isolate you for a one-on-one interview. Or you may give a series of interviews on the same subject over a period of hours or days. The result is that you may talk about the same subject so many times that you'll be tempted to say something new or different—if only to avoid boring yourself. Don't confuse the need for repetition with the need to revise. As far as every new interviewer (or audience) is concerned, you are presenting to them for the first time. Struggle against the tedium and stay with your agenda—as long as it works.

I get a lot of heat sometimes for training people to meet the press. Once I was speaking at a journalism-school seminar, and one of the young people stood up and accused me of doing something immoral by teaching people how to answer questions from the press. It was as if I were somehow advising them not to tell the truth.

And I said, "We always advise our clients to tell the truth. But the thing that disturbs me most is that you are here in journalism school learning how to ask the questions, yet you would deny a person the right to learn how to answer those questions. Remember, this is America. What's fair for one is fair for the other."

That ended the conversation.

YOUR BILL OF RIGHTS

Anybody who wants to improve his communication skills has that right. Without training, some very talented and intelligent people would avoid all media situations because they fear embarrassment. A business executive needs training because the press will selectively edit anything he says. It may all be the truth, but only part of it may be relevant. Does a business executive have the right not to answer a question? Yes. Does he have the right to choose his words and not use the reporter's words? Yes. Does he have the right to learn how to rehearse his responses before he walks out there with a bunch of lights and cameras pointed at him? Yes. Does he have the right to understand the technical nature of the interview-editing process? Yes. Does he have the right to know what to wear on camera? Yes. Should he be presumed innocent until proven guilty even if he refuses to answer certain questions? Yes.

Remember, when you go into a press situation, it's a natural adversarial relationship. The reporter is a professional. Don't get into the ring if you're a rank amateur.

EPILOGUE

If you've read this far, you know by now that one of the themes of this book is that we're all human. We make mistakes. We're vulnerable. We're not perfect. The thing that interferes most with communications, at times, is our attempt to prove that we're not vulnerable—to keep a stiff upper lip or to appear macho in the face of imagined attacks. Here's a final lesson I learned from one of the greatest entertainers of all time—Judy Garland.

In her twilight days, Judy was so ill that she often couldn't complete a show. Alcohol and pills had taken their toll. Her voice was almost gone and she had trouble controlling her vibrato. When I met her, I was so shaken by her voice in rehearsal and her appearance that I couldn't understand why she had such a loyal following. But anyone who saw her in concert understood her magic. The audience identified with her "humanness." They identified with her frailties. They understood her vulnerability. When she sang at Carnegie Hall and tried to hit the high notes in "Over the Rainbow," twenty-eight hundred people were praying for her to make it. She understood that.

If you can get the audience to pull for you, you'll always win. After all, audiences are just like you. They're human. They care. They're sympathetic. They're supportive. The audience wants you to succeed. Show them that you care about them.

Try your best, just as Judy did every time she went on stage. Draw strength from others. An awareness of your own vulnerability and the vulnerability of others will make you a better and more human communicator. And only a human communicator can become a master communicator.

USER'S GUIDE

CHAPTER 1: THE FIRST SEVEN SECONDS

Summary

• We make a quick assessment of other people within seven seconds of first meeting them. What sort of instant impression do you make on others?

• Food, shelter, and clothing have always been listed as the prime essentials of the human survival kit. Communication belongs in that grouping.

• Good communication starts with good conversation. It is an art comprising listening, reacting, enthusiasm, empathy, and a mutual understanding of thought.

• Communication is a process of shared comprehension.

• The common denominator to success is the understanding and efficient application of the basic principles of communication.

• Implicit or openly stated in every job description is the requirement to be an effective communicator.

• The ten most common problems in communication are:

1. Initial rapport is not established with listeners.
2. Body movements are stiff or wooden.
3. Material is presented intellectually, not involving the audience emotionally.

4. Speaker seems uncomfortable due to fear of failure.
5. Eye contact and facial expression are poorly utilized.
6. Humor is lacking.
7. Speaker's intentions are not made clear due to improper preparation.
8. Silence is not used for impact.
9. Energy is low, resulting in inappropriate pitch pattern, speech rate, and volume.
10. Language and material are boring.

Questions/Exercises for Discussion and Reflection

• Practice reading people's nonverbal communication by: (1) watching television with the sound turned off; (2) from a distance, observing people talking on public telephones; (3) discreetly studying the interactions of people seated near you at other tables in a restaurant. How many different emotions can you identify by watching their facial expressions? Whether they are talking or listening, what do you interpret about them from their body language? Try to guess the nature of their relationship to those they engage in conversation.

• On a small index card, write down the list of the ten most common communication problems. Bring the list to a business meeting, speech, class, or local government meeting. How many of the problems do you detect in anyone who is speaking? Based on the principles of this book, what advice would you give the speaker to remedy his or her communication problems?

CHAPTER 2: TELEVISION CHANGED THE RULES

Summary

• Television has set the style of a modern communicator—relaxed, informal, crisp, quick, and entertaining.

• Television's fast pace has made us an impatient society. Make your point quickly and be interesting.

• Using mental images enlivens communication. If you can

see a picture in your mind and describe it, others will stay tuned in. See it and say it.

• In the television age, we are all broadcasters. Each person is his own message, whatever medium he chooses.

Questions/Exercises for Discussion and Reflection

• Develop your ability to use colorful language by comparing one thing to another, using the term "like a . . ." For instance, the poet Carl Sandburg said, "Life is like an onion: you peel it off one layer at a time, and sometimes you weep." If you were to make a comparison using the phrase "Life is like a ————," how would you fill in the blank? Think of something memorable that happened to you and complete the thought "That experience was like a ————." Or, recall a strong emotional reaction you had and apply it to finish the thought "It made me feel like a ————." Have fun with this— be a little outrageous, exaggerate, or use "poetic license" in your word choices. However, try to avoid using clichés. See if you can use language in a fresh way. You'll enjoy doing this more if you ask a friend to brainstorm with you about how to fill in the blanks, or if you turn it into a party game involving a group of people.

CHAPTER 3: YOU ARE THE MESSAGE

Summary

• Take an inventory and list personal assets that help you communicate—physical appearance, energy, rate of speech, pitch and tone of voice, animation and gestures, humor, and so forth.

• There is no established fault-free "communication posture." You have to be yourself at your best without any drastic changes in personality. Nobody can play you as well as you can.

• Once you have reached a successful level of communication, you do not change or adapt your essential self to different audiences or different media.

- All communication is a dialogue, whether it be with one person or a thousand and one.
- A good communicator takes responsibility for the flow of communication, whether speaking or listening. Don't rely on people to accommodate themselves to you. You are in charge of every communication situation you're in.
- Audiences tend to respond to visual signals over verbal signals sent out by the speaker. If the speaker is somber and uncomfortable, his message becomes negative, too.
- If you must read a speech, make it conversational. Look at the audience whenever you can. Don't make sentences too long. Pace your reading so that your eyes are up at the end of a sentence, and never rush the speech. You want to be an interesting speaker, not just a good reader.
- You are the message. Bring personality and enthusiasm to your speech. This will enhance the message.

Questions/Exercises for Discussion and Reflection
- How would you describe the "composite" you? How would you describe the "composite message" sent by your favorite entertainer, coworker, friend, or relative? What can you learn about broadening your composite message from studying the composite messages of people you admire?
- Test your powers of observation and description by walking into a room, looking around for seven seconds, then closing your eyes and telling someone else everything you can recall about the room—colors, textures, inanimate objects, the expressions on people's faces, such as warm, friendly, hostile, etc. Developing your ability to quickly absorb what's going on around you will enable you to communicate better under many different circumstances.
- Make a list of everyone you have contact with on a given day. How would each person score on the "guest meter"? What kind of a guest might they be at a party or on a television talk show? How do you rate as a guest? What might others (or you) do to become more interesting, likable, and informed?
- Think of a time when you should have spoken up but

either didn't or, when it was already too late, tried to speak. How might you have communicated better in that circumstance?

• Read aloud from a speech or an article while standing in front of a mirror. How much eye contact can you manage, using the techniques in this book?

CHAPTER 4: INSTINCTS AND RULES

Summary

• Many public speaking courses are based on outdated approaches. Today we use our senses to observe and develop the process of communication. It's visual and intuitive. It's watching, feeling, sensing, hearing. It's the new age of communication.

• A forced emotion convinces no one. An emotion triggered by a thought and resulting in natural expression is the beginning of mutual acceptance of ideas.

• Smiling originates first in the brain, then on the face.

• Fifteen minutes of practice a day in voice improvement not only adds quality to the voice but also improves pronunciation, articulation, and inflection.

• "Tape and ape" the best pros, not to mimic but to develop range and vocal variety.

• If you care about your subject, your listeners also will care.

• In every communications situation—one-on-one or in a group—ask yourself: What am I feeling here? If you sense that people are not tuned in to you, don't waste your time pushing out ideas.

• We all have the capability to "read" and sense what's happening with others. This ability is every bit as accurate as the eyes and ears. It can be your edge in negotiations.

• Other people's perception of you is their reality. You must be aware of their assessment in order to effect good communication.

• In the dinosaur age of communications, you "projected"

first and observed your audience later, if at all. In the new age, you observe what's going on first and project afterward.

Questions/Exercises for Discussion and Reflection

• If you have access to a video camera and have a friend willing to interview you, record a discussion where the camera focuses on you while your friend asks you about your hobbies, your interests, or a range of issues drawn from whatever section of the newspaper you most enjoy reading. Watch the playback of the interview. How expressive were you in your verbal and nonverbal communication? If you didn't know the person on the screen, would you still have enjoyed watching the interview?

• Tape-record your end of a telephone conversation. How does your voice sound? Is your pitch too high? What adjustments are advisable to make your voice more attractive? Using the suggestions in this book, work on your volume, pitch, inflection, emphasis, or other vocal characteristics. Then, compare how you sound when you record yourself again speaking on the telephone.

• Reread the list of tips for opening a speech or making remarks before any group. Try implementing at least one of the suggestions for quickly getting the audience's attention.

• Each time you casually greet someone by asking "How are you?" reflect for a moment what you "absorbed" about the other person, based on his or her response.

CHAPTER 5: POOR RECEPTION

Summary

• People are inefficient listeners. Tests indicate that after listening to a ten-minute oral presentation, the average listener retains half of what was said. Within forty-eight hours, that drops another 50 percent to 25 percent retention level. By the end of a week, the retention level drops to 10 percent or less.

• As you develop your listening habits, listen for intent as well as content. If something sounds out of sync, ask for clarification.

• Human communication goes through three phases: speaking (transmission), analyzing (information processing), and listening (reception). Listen without overanalyzing; listen without interrupting the speaker, or you may short-circuit the listening process.

• Most of us talk more than we need to. If most of the time you talk more than you listen, you're probably failing in your communication.

Questions/Exercises for Discussion and Reflection

• To identify how good you are as a listener, apply the "I.D." test. "I" is for "interruption" and "D" is for "distraction." When you're listening, how often do you interrupt others or get distracted? Try to minimize both of these blocks to better understanding.

CHAPTER 6: THE FOUR ESSENTIALS OF A GREAT COMMUNICATOR

Summary

• *Be prepared:* (1) Your listeners must have confidence that you know what you're talking about; (2) your listeners should feel that you know more about the subject than they do; (3) it must be apparent that you spent time preparing your subject and analyzing your audience; (4) there must be a purpose to your message—to inform, to entertain, to inspire, or all three; and (5) you may be facing a hostile or skeptical audience. (Before a hostile audience, you will need to show understanding of all sides of an issue; before supportive audiences, you will need to reaffirm shared values.)

• See chapter for checklist of tips for preparing and delivering a speech.

• Others take their cues from you. So try to relax. Keep things in perspective. Don't overreact.

• Maintain your sense of humor. Take your work seriously but not yourself or human foibles.

• Avoid arrogance, lecturing others, and similarly disagreeable behavior. Focus more on empathizing than criticizing.

• *Make others comfortable.*

• *Be committed:* If you know what you're saying, know why you are saying it, and care about what you are saying, you will say it well.

• Know when you have to be good and when someone else's opinion of you counts; be yourself but at your best; always believe in what you're saying.

• *Be interesting:* The Brotherhood of Boredom has had its day in communication. It will be tolerated less and less in boardrooms and meeting halls.

• You can add substance to communication and still project a style of delivery that is impressive to your listeners. Don't be limited by the traditional scope of your subject. Think of analogies from other fields that can enliven your material and help the audience remember your key points.

• At least 30 percent of all your reading should be outside your own field. This will broaden your perspective and knowledge.

Questions/Exercises for Discussion and Reflection

• Next time you speak before a group, ask a friend in the audience to take notes on a single sheet of paper divided horizontally into four parts, with each section headed by one of the four essentials of a great communicator. Ask your friend to write comments on how you fulfill each of the four essentials.

CHAPTER 7: THE MAGIC BULLET

Summary

• The "magic bullet" of personal communication is the quality of being likable.

• The "like factor" in politics can swing elections. In business, it can build relationships among employees on all levels.

- Likability is difficult to define or to teach, but the basic positives that reside in the likable person are (1) optimism, (2) concern about the welfare of other people, (3) ability to see the opportunity in every difficulty, (4) ability to handle stress, (5) ability to laugh easily, especially at himself, and (6) ability to perform at his best in crises and at his humblest in prosperity.
- To be a master communicator, one must add likability to the four essentials of being prepared, comfortable, committed, and interesting.

Questions/Exercises for Discussion and Reflection
- On which "likable" measures are you strongest? Weakest? What adjustments to your behavior or attitude could make you more likable? Discuss this with someone you respect and trust.

CHAPTER 8: THE DOUBLE-EDGED SWORD

Summary
- Emotion is the double-edged sword of communication. It is a constructive and powerful force of persuasion when genuine and positive, but mistrusted when negative and insincere.
- You reveal yourself to your audience through visible and expressed emotions. Your audience then knows who you are and why you're there.
- People want to see a speaker's range of emotions expressed with commitment and colored with nuances of humor, sincerity, energy, and enthusiasm.
- To an audience, there are head issues and heart issues. A good communicator increases his likability by varying cold facts with warm, genuine emotion. Facts provide information; emotion provides interpretation.
- Successful managers of the future will be "bilingual," that is, comfortable with and adept at using the cultural styles of both men and women.
- A basic formula for professional success includes (1) integrity, (2) talent, and (3) good communication skills.

Questions/Exercises for Discussion and Reflection

• For you, what are three "head" issues and three "heart" issues? Try discussing these issues with other people (particularly if they disagree with you). Listen for and observe the emotion that comes out during the discussion. Is the emotion you express appropriate for the points you want to make, and are others displaying their emotions to advantage? Another way to study emotion is to watch a television talk show that features hosts and guests debating controversial social and political issues. How do you feel about the emotion projected by each speaker?

CHAPTER 9: BEYOND CHARISMA: CONTROL OF THE ATMOSPHERE

Summary

• Charismatic personalities never doubt their ability to add value to a situation, whether that value comes from the prestige of their presence, the quality of their knowledge and experience, the projection of their optimism and enthusiasm, or their distinct personality and style.

• Charisma is the ability to cause others to respond to you, as opposed to your responding to others. It is personal confidence, as opposed to the confidence imparted by a job title or other trappings of power.

• Those who control the atmosphere are risk takers with an aura of unpredictability—in essence, fearlessness without arrogance.

• Winners are thermostats—they set the right temperature. Losers are thermometers—they go up and down according to the climate others set.

• A charisma quotient measures self-confidence, leadership qualities, definable goals, control of one's life, and the attributes of being comfortable and making others feel comfortable.

• A successful communicator is prepared to go into any kind of communication process and change the flow of thought.

This is control of the atmosphere through assertion of skill, personality, knowledge, and belief, and through the energy of enthusiasm.

- In all successful first meetings a comfort level is quickly established. During this sizing-up process, lines of communication are established which insure a comfortable process of conversation.

- Good speakers control space (how and where they move and gesture). They also control time (rate of speech, length of remarks, pauses, silence).

- People who control the atmosphere don't act threatened, frightened, or superior. They treat everybody with the same comfort level and goodwill.

- A high control-of-the-atmosphere quotient reflects total control of time, space, eye contact, voice, state of mind, attitude, flow of dialogue, absorb-project balance, and personal feelings.

Questions/Exercises for Discussion and Reflection
Attend a meeting in your town of any civic group (Parent-Teacher Association or school board, government body, court session, local club, fellowship committee at a house of worship, etc.). Who among the participants communicate with confidence and control, regardless of their title or status? What do you notice about the way they carry and express themselves? If you have the opportunity, speak up about an issue that concerns you. Are you able to make your points in a way that holds the attention of the audience? Benchmark the performance of those you observe (or yourself) against the control-of-the-atmosphere factors listed in the chapter.

CHAPTER 10: AN OUNCE OF ENERGY IS WORTH A POUND OF TECHNIQUE

Summary

• With the right kind of energy, you're focused, you're interested in others, and you're absorbing what others are telling you. You project enthusiasm.

• A good communicator's energy is perceived as a "life force" vitality, a vigor exemplified by successful professionals in the business, sports, and media worlds.

• Properly focused energy comes across as a magnetic intensity, an inner flame that says, "I am committed, I believe, I want to tell you."

Questions/Exercises for Discussion and Reflection

Try this experiment in the transforming power of positive energy. The next time you get to the head of the line at a ticket counter or ask anyone for information, greet the person with a sincere hello and a smile. Watch how the other person reacts to your friendly energy. Consider how a more energetic approach might work in a situation where you need to gain the goodwill or help of others.

CHAPTER 11: LIGHTEN UP, YOU'RE WEARING EVERYBODY OUT

Summary

• According to executive recruiters, seven out of ten people lose their jobs because of personality conflicts, not because of lack of skills.

• For middle management and up, the primary criteria for advancement are communication and motivation skills.

• The essential responsibility of any employee is to be positive, enthusiastic, and friendly.

• To lighten up doesn't mean you become a comedian, but it

does mean appreciating humor and seeing the lighter side in stressful situations.

• The six Rs of humor are research, relevance, rhythm, rehearsal, relaxation, and risk.

Questions/Exercises for Discussion and Reflection

The next time you feel yourself or someone else getting upset about something, try to control the situation by consciously de-escalating the tension. How might you put what is happening into a lighter, less serious perspective? Gauge your reaction by asking yourself this question: In two weeks, two months, or two years, will all this seem as important as it does now? If the answer is no, what can you do to smile, relax, make others more comfortable, and maybe even add a little levity to the situation?

CHAPTER 12: OKAY, AILES, FIX ME: THE AILES METHOD/COURSE

Summary

• No one can manufacture an "image" for anyone. All a consultant can do is advise and guide you on how to capitalize on your personal assets.

• Acting isn't the skill required for effective communication of your own ideas. Acting is when someone hands you a script and asks you to be somebody other than who you really are.

• Performing demands that you be yourself. Acting is a passing illusion; performing is the "real you" at the gut and mind level reflecting true commitment.

• "At your best" is a simple checklist of factors: physical appearance, energy, speech rate, pitch, tone, phrasing, gestures, eye contact, and holding audience interest.

• Research has shown that audience interpretations of speaker messages are determined 55 percent by the speaker's nonverbal communication (facial expression, body language), 38 percent by the speaker's vocal quality (tone, pitch, volume, variation), and only 7 percent by the literal words.

- Overall, audiences remember concepts (idea clusters formed by the words) and emotional expression (as communicated through the eyes, face, voice, and body).

Questions/Exercises for Discussion and Reflection

In your personal estimation or according to a colleague or friend, how consistently are you communicating at your best, measured by the checklist of factors listed in the chapter? Are you willing to make an effort to improve? Whom do you know who might benefit from applying the checklist to themselves and how might you make them aware of it? Here are two options for getting feedback on your communication skills: (1) The next time you address an audience, if the occasion is appropriate, ask the person in charge of the meeting if he or she wants to distribute a brief evaluation form for your listeners to fill in about you, containing the checklist items. Be sure the form is distributed by the chairperson and is explained as coming from the sponsoring organization—not from you (you don't want to seem too self-serving). (2) Another way to get feedback is to sit for a videotaped mock job interview conducted by a friend—whether or not you're looking for a job. As you watch the playback, would *you* hire you? Choose at least one aspect of your communication skills that you'll consciously work on this month.

CHAPTER 13: EVEN HEROES GET SCARED

Summary

- In a poll of human fears, twice as many people were more afraid of speaking in public than of dying. Fear of failure and embarrassment are the main reasons people don't do things in life.
- Insecure communicators usually see themselves as worse speakers than they really are.
- There are two kinds of anxiety that may affect how we address an individual (or group): external anxiety caused by frightening outside situations that might occur, and internal

anxiety that results from illness. Less than 2 percent of people actually suffer from internal anxiety.

• The greatest antidotes to fear are preparation of material and use of energy in delivery.

• Since you are the message, you must view yourself in a short-term and a long-term way. Short-term, as in a speech, use everything in your power at the moment and forge ahead. Long-term, improve yourself constantly to bring forth a successful lifetime. Do not confuse the two.

Questions/Exercises for Discussion and Reflection

Think about your greatest fears. Picture yourself in front of an audience and consider the absolute worst consequences of your showing fearful behavior to others. Could you survive the worst and would the audience "forgive" you (or even care that much)? If communicating in certain situations gives you the jitters, minimize your anxiety and be fair to yourself by preparing what you're going to say as much in advance as possible. If you make a mistake, don't fuss over it. Get back to your topic. Work up the courage to put yourself in one communication circumstance you've been dreading. When you're in front of your audience, don't try to be perfect. Just focus on getting your message across. Once you complete your presentation, how reasonable or awful were the fears that earlier bothered you? What reaction did you get from the audience?

CHAPTER 14: "MAKING IT" IN GRANDMA'S EYES

Summary

• The safest course in dealing with the press is not to make "off the record" statements. The only thing off the record is what you don't say.

• If you have wisecracking instincts, keep them in check around the media.

• You have an obligation to help the press by providing true and complete information. But don't be cornered into meeting a reporter's deadline if it forces you to provide incomplete or unsubstantiated facts.

Questions/Exercises for Discussion and Reflection
If you were to conduct an interview with the press, what subject(s) could you speak about with authority? How would you prepare yourself for meeting the press? What topics would you prefer to keep private and how would you respond if a reporter confronted you with those topics?

CHAPTER 15: MEDIA TACTICS: SCORING ON DEFENSE

Summary
- Check out all over-the-phone media requests for information. You need to check out the reporter, what he wants, and why he might want it.
- With the media, you are always on defense, but if you do it right, you occasionally score.
- Never go into a media interview unprepared. Discuss the interview in advance with a public relations professional, a media trainer, or other trusted counsel. Reverse your roles: If you were the journalist, what questions would you ask?
- Have an agenda with at least three major points you want to mention in the interview. The most common mistake made by people who are interviewed is that they wait for the reporter to ask questions related to the major points they are prepared to make. That may never happen.
- The medium determines the message. Newspaper interviews allow you time to explain. Radio and TV interviews require "headline" answers.
- Never assume that your agenda and the reporter's agenda are alike. You have a prepared point of view, but the reporter has a series of questions that may go beyond the scope of your agenda. Early in the interview you must try to build a bridge between the two agendas.
- You are not obliged to reveal confidential information, but

don't dismiss the query with "No comment." Give a rational explanation as to the proprietary nature of some of your information.

• In news interviews, be friendly, be brief, be direct, and be positive.

• Avoid jargon, speak plainly, and use examples and illustrations expressed in laymen's terms.

• Stay composed at all times. Part of the reporter's armament is to throw you off balance, so stay calm and stick to your point of view with short, clear answers.

• Whether it's a TV, radio, or print interview, say what you have to say, then stop. It's the reporter's problem to come up with the next question. Generally, the tougher the question, the shorter your answer should be.

• Dress conservatively. Don't let your wardrobe overwhelm your words.

• A practical formula for interviews runs thusly: $Q = A + 1$. A question is asked (Q). Reply with a brief answer (A). Then add a point or points (+ 1), preferably from your prepared agenda.

• You can ask a reporter if you can review his text of the interview, but don't request changes in his writing style.

• The more inflammatory the journalist, the cooler you should be.

• If a reporter uses negative, hypothetical, or incorrect words in a question, don't legitimize them by repeating them in your answer.

• Develop three levels, or "tiers," for each answer, to the most challenging questions that may be asked by a reporter: Tier A is a short summary of your position. Tier B is a concrete example or fact to back up your summary. Tier C is a further elaboration and another supporting statement. If a reporter pushes you further, go back to tier A.

• Audiences have a short attention span, so cut to the heart of the matter.

• In all interviews, don't give in to pressure to go beyond the bounds of your stated position.

Questions/Exercises for Discussion and Reflection

Ask a friend or colleague to conduct a mock media interview with you on a subject related to your work or interests. Make a list of at least three proactive points you'd want to communicate if you met with the press. Play devil's advocate and also list the areas where you might be vulnerable to criticism or tough probing. How skillful are you at implementing the $Q = A + 1$ formula explained in this book? Ask the interviewer for feedback (or, if you've recorded the interview, come to your own conclusions). How successful were you at presenting a positive composite message, one in which your style and substance worked well together? Did you say anything quotable? Returning to the concept of the "guest meter," where would you rate (boring, okay, interesting, memorable, book this person back)? Did you say or do anything you'd regret if the interview were broadcast or printed? Review this chapter again and pinpoint areas where you might improve your media interviewing skills.

EPILOGUE

Summary

• Remember: We're all human and vulnerable. Show that side of yourself to others and they'll be more sympathetic to you.

Questions/Exercises for Discussion and Reflection

Arrogance defeats likability. Speakers succeed only if audiences allow them to succeed. This will happen only if the speaker sincerely tries to communicate with the audience, as opposed to acting full of self-importance. Does arrogance ever creep into your communication? Remember: Audiences will respond more favorably to a genuine, human approach.

NOTES

1. Eugene B. McDaniel with James Johnson, *Scars and Stripes* (Philadelphia and New York: A. J. Holman Company, 1975), p. 40.
2. Nick Jordan, "The Face of Feeling," *Psychology Today* 20, no. 1 (January 1986), p. 8.
3. Robert O. Skovgard, ed., *Openings* (Dayton, Ohio: The Executive Speaker Co., 1984), p. 24.
4. Ibid., p. 14.
5. Ibid., p. 4.
6. Ibid., p. 2.
7. Gerald Gardner, *All the President's Wits: The Power of Presidential Humor* (New York: Beech Tree Books, William Morrow Publishing, 1986), p. 222.
8. Ibid., p. 137.
9. Ibid., p. 37.
10. Ibid., p. 20.
11. James Brady, "In Step with Perry King," *Parade*, February 8, 1987, p. 22.
12. Robert O. Skovgard, "Summaries and Closings," *The Executive Speaker* 7, no. 1 (January 1986), p. 9.
13. Skovgard, *Openings*, p. 36.
14. Ibid., p. 26.
15. Lou Cannon, *Reporting: An Inside View* (Sacramento: California Journal Press, 1977), p. 5.
16. Thomas Griffith, *How True: A Skeptic's Guide to Believing the News* (Boston: Little, Brown & Company, 1974), p. 7.
17. Bill Hunter, "The Softening of Business Communication," *IABC Communication World 2*, no. 2 (February 1985), p. 29.

INDEX

ABOUT AILES
COMMUNICATIONS

TRAINING

Ailes Communications provides communications, leadership, and media training programs developed by the authors of *You Are the Message*, company founder Roger Ailes and his longtime colleague, ACI president Jon Kraushar. ACI trains executives, authors, and leaders in many other fields seeking to most effectively get their messages through to a variety of important audiences, including customers, stockholders, the press, and government officials. Private training courses are custom-designed for each individual or organization.

RESEARCH

Ailes Communications offers a full range of quantitative and qualitative research services. ACI creates and executes research projects that range from advertising testing to message and positioning analyses. The research results are presented as raw data, supplemented by analyses and recommendations compiled by the ACI team.

STRATEGIC CONSULTING

For the past twenty-five years, the strategic consulting services of Ailes Communications have been highly sought-after by some of the nation's most prominent organizations and leaders. ACI's team synthesizes its corporate, entertainment, and political experience to provide clients with unique and innovative solutions to communications problems. Strategic projects can be undertaken on a retainer or project basis.

PRODUCTION

The film and video production capabilities of Ailes Communications are well known throughout the television and corporate communities. Projects range from advertising production to corporate videos to broadcast television projects like the CBS special *The All-Star Salute to Our Troops* (1991) or the syndicated "Rush Limbaugh: The Television Show."

For more information about *You Are the Message* and Ailes Communications, please call 1 800 CEO-READ (1 800 236-7323). ACI's fax line is 1 800 231-7323. To insure a prompt reply to your fax, please include your name, address, phone, fax number, and the nature of your inquiry.

ABOUT THE AUTHORS

Roger Ailes is president of the NBC-owned cable television channels CNBC and America's Talking, where he hosts an interview program called "Straight Forward." An Emmy Award–winner, he is a partner in and executive producer of "Rush Limbaugh: The Television Show." Ailes' many other acclaimed productions include *The All-Star Salute to Our Troops* following the Gulf War, and *Television and the Presidency.* A political media adviser in three winning presidential campaigns, he also founded Ailes Communications of New York, consultants to corporations and entertainment companies.

Jon Kraushar is president and chief operating officer of Ailes Communications of New York, which provides executive training, advertising and marketing strategies, research, and production for a variety of business and entertainment clients. He is a former award-winning newspaper journalist and television news writer and producer.